FIVE MAKERS OF THE
NEW TESTAMENT

FIVE MAKERS OF THE NEW TESTAMENT

by

DONALD COGGAN
Archbishop of York

HODDER AND STOUGHTON

For
ANN
who teaches
and
RUTH
who seeks to heal

CONTENTS

FOREWORD

CERTAIN basic convictions have prompted the writing of this book. First, the conviction that twentieth-century men and women desperately need the message of the New Testament. Secondly, that multitudes of them respond to a preaching of that message which is alive, informed, and relevant. Thirdly, that those who preach need constantly the stimulus of books which are not necessarily highly technical but which are expository, and which point the way to the bearing of first-century writings on modern belief and life. Fourthly, that we cannot do enough to help those people, clerical and lay, who week by week, in pulpit and in classes of various kinds, set themselves to the task of teaching and evangelism. It is such that I have had in mind in writing this book.

Part of these chapters was given as the Maynard-Chapman Divinity Lectures at Westfield College, London, in 1960, and I am grateful to the Principal, Dr. Kathleen Chesney, both for her kind hospitality and for her request that the Lectures should see the light of day. The Lecture on the Book of the Revelation called for more extended treatment, if only because the Apocalypse is so difficult a book and so little understood. The opportunity to elaborate the Lecture came when I lectured to groups of clergy in Cambridge and Ireland in September, 1960. The popular style has been retained, and I have not sought to disguise the fact that I was speaking to ministers of the Word.

If a reading of *Five Makers of the New Testament* acts as a stimulus to further study of these five men and of those others who gave us our canonical writings, and if this study leads on to more vigorous and better preaching, I shall indeed be happy.

DONALD EBOR:

Bishopthorpe,
York.

Feast of the Conversion of
St. Paul, 1962.

I

ST. PAUL

IF St. Paul could come and stand beside me here today just as he was 1900 years ago, what kind of man should I introduce you to? "A man of moderate stature, with curly hair and scanty, crooked legs, blue eyes and large knit eyebrows, long nose, and he was full of the grace and pity of the Lord, sometimes having the appearance of a man, but sometimes looking like an angel." So runs the well-known description which occurs in the *Acts of Paul and Thecla*, a document which may ultimately go back to the first century in parts. Certainly the description is so unflattering as to bear the marks of truth! We can recognise a typical little Jew, perhaps, at first glance, not over-impressive. St. Paul, indeed, himself records that his enemies said that while he could, from a distance, write a snorter of a letter, he was not much to look at nor was he much good as an orator (II Corinthians 10, 10). He must have been pretty tough physically. Anybody who could emerge alive after the kind of ordeals through which he passed must have had a body like steel. "Are they servants of Christ? I am a better one—I am talking like a madman—with far greater labours, far more imprisonments, with countless beatings, and often near death. Five times I have received at the hands of the Jews the forty lashes less one. Three times I have been beaten with rods; once I was stoned. Three times I have been shipwrecked; a night and a day I have been adrift at sea; on frequent journeys, in danger from rivers, danger from robbers, danger from my own people, danger from Gentiles, danger in the city, danger in the wilderness, danger at sea, danger from false brethren; in toil and hardship, through many a sleepless night, in hunger and thirst, often without food, in cold and exposure. And, apart from other things, there is the daily pressure upon me of my anxiety for all the churches." (II Corinthians 11, 23 ff.). No wonder he could write: "I bear in my body the marks of the Lord Jesus" (Galatians 6, 17) —a reference, no doubt, to the weals of the lash whose marks he would carry to his dying day and in which he rejoiced, for he regarded them as the brand marks which his Master Jesus had put upon His willing slave (*doulos* was his favourite word for his relationship to his Lord). "I buffet my body and make it my slave" (I Corinthians 9, 27). He knew the meaning of self-discipline.

Nevertheless, that body of his had its sicknesses —and no wonder! What precisely the trouble was we do not know —epilepsy, malaria, eye-trouble have all been suggested. Who could endure what he did, and travel through the low-lying and malaria-infested places of Asia Minor, and escape unscathed? He had to write to the Galatians (6, 11) in great big characters; he could not perceive that the man who gave orders for him to be hit on the mouth was the High Priest, in spite of all his official garments (Acts 23, 1–9). It looks as if bad sight was at least part of his physical trouble. He describes the body variously as a tent in which one groans (II Corinthians 5, 2); an earthen vessel (II Corinthians 4, 7); a body of humiliation (Philippians 3, 21). The trouble that came to him and which hindered his work, but which became to him a very means of grace, could be described as a stake, a pointed piece of wood, which went into his flesh (II Corinthians 12, 7). Tough he might be. Tough, indeed, he must have been. But he knew what physical anguish could be. "One of the most lasting impressions," wrote Adolf Deissmann, "derived from [my two journeys over the routes travelled by St. Paul] is my unspeakable amazement at the purely physical accomplishment of St. Paul the traveller . . . Strength is made perfect in weakness!" (*St. Paul: A Study in Social and Religious History* p. 66).

Physical anguish — yes, and mental anguish too. Here is a sensitive soul, if ever there was one. Deeply affectionate, he can, without any suggestion of self-adulation, compare himself to a nurse (I Thessalonians 2, 7), a mother who travailed (Galatians 4, 19) and so on. He writes of his longing for the companionship of his children in Christ from whom, for one reason or another, he is separated. The run-away slave, Onesimus, who meets St. Paul at Rome and through him meets Christ is "begotten in my bonds". The terms of endearment which bestrew his letters are the language of a strong man whose emotions run deep.

"For the sake of Christ Jesus my Lord," he writes (Philippians 3, 8), "I have suffered the loss of all things." What lies behind that pregnant sentence? It may well be his disinheritance, because of his conversion, from all that he held dearest in his home life. His parents were strict and orthodox Jews who from his earliest days brought up their son in the ways of a rigid Pharisaism. Or, at least, if they did not wholly succeed, it was not for want of trying. "Circumcised on the eighth day, of the people of Israel, of the tribe of Benjamin, a Hebrew born of Hebrews, as to the Law a Pharisee" (Philippians 3, 5) — what could be more orthodox than that? Taught in the law almost from infancy, nurtured on the Old Testament in the synagogue, sitting at the feet of Gamaliel at Jerusalem, moved by a passionate devotion to his people, his inborn *Jewishness* comes out even in those letters which were written long after his conversion to Christianity. Indeed, the passages which, by reason of their allegorical nature, are to us Western Christians most difficult to understand (for

example, 1 Corinthians 10, 1–11, and Galatians 4, 21 ff.)
are (if an irreverent phrase may be used) the hangover of
Pharisaic exegetical method used in Christian exposition.
You cannot, even with a radical conversion, totally
eradicate his orthodox Jewish ways of thought. Not for
naught was he "extremely zealous . . . for the traditions of
my fathers" (Galatians 1, 14).

But there were other strands than the Hebraic which
went to the make-up of this complicated character. St.
Paul had an "hospitable mind", and not a little of that
"hospitable-ness" was due to the fact that he was brought
up in a city in which Jews were very much in the minority.
Tarsus was a place in which fresh winds constantly blew.
Saul's parents might have said, with justification from the
point of view of strict monotheists, that they were winds
putrid with the stench of polytheism and heresies of all
sorts. But *winds* they were, and they could not but affect
the mind of young Saul. Those charming pagans with
whom he rubbed shoulders every day; those games which
he watched, albeit with a twinge of conscience for his
parents had forbidden such acts; those statues which
adorned the temples and which owed their lines to the
beauty that was Greece; those open sea-ways, free of
robbers since the Romans had cleared them—which en-
abled him to travel to Palestine on his lawful occasions;
that *pax Romana* which embraced almost the whole
world—these, and a thousand other things, impinged on
the developing mind of young Saul. They made him not
one whit less loyal to his Jewish inheritance. But they
caused him to ally himself whole-heartedly with that strong
strand of Jewish tradition which was not wholly exclusive
in its outlook, but which longed for the day when the
nations of the world would find their way to Zion and,
leaving their polytheisms behind, would acknowledge
Yahweh as their King for ever. (See, for example, Isaiah

49, 60 and 66.) Jew though he was, he found much in Hellenism to which he could respond with delight; and his Roman citizenship was something of which he was extremely proud. He found himself the heir of three cultures, the Jewish, the Greek, and the Roman. He was a world-citizen.

And he was a coming man. With two universities behind him, Tarsus and Jerusalem, he found that people would look twice when he passed. He had, on his own admission, "advanced in Judaism beyond many of my own age among my people" (Galatians 1, 14). The religious leaders of the nation were not slow in granting him letters to the synagogues (Acts 9, 2) to stamp out a miserable heresy which was gaining ground in Palestine. The adherents of this heresy said they belonged to *the Way* —itself a startling claim! They held that the Messiah *had come*, not only was to come. They held that He had died a felon's death —and risen again. Nonsense —and dangerous nonsense at that. The thing was spreading like a plague. Who better than young Saul to stamp it out?

He went to the task with a will, "breathing out threats and murder against the disciples of the Lord" (Acts 9, 1). As he interrogated group after group, he learned a great deal, and the more he learned the less he liked it. Who was this Jesus for whom they made such preposterous claims? There had been false Messiahs before and doubtless there would be again. What was this new Law of love which He had proclaimed? Was not the Law of Moses good enough? What was this new fellowship meal in which His disciples shared? Was not the Passover feast good enough for any religious Jew? What were they teaching about circumcision, and the rites by which entry might be made into the assembly of the believers? Was it necessary, or was it not? And then, Stephen! Bah! The man had deserved what he got —death by stoning. Before long there would be others

15

stoned as he had been—the best way to deal with such heretics! Meanwhile his job was to bind all whom he found belonging to what they called *the Way*, and to bring them to Jerusalem. That would soon put paid to that little heresy, and Saul himself could return to the quieter paths of Jewish scholarship and Rabbinic leadership.

But it wasn't quite as simple as that. Saul was having trouble in sleeping at night. He would just be dropping off when he would hear the voice of Stephen: "Lord Jesus, receive my spirit. Lord, lay not this sin to their charge" (Acts 7, 59, 60). He would see his face, as it had been the face of an angel. He had never seen a man die like that. What was the secret? His mind, now awake and alert, would go over those periods of interrogation which he had just held with the followers of Jesus. There was a strange calm about them which he had not noticed elsewhere; a depth of fellowship which seemed to make barriers of class and sex irrelevant in a way new to him. And they seemed to be in touch with this Jesus of Nazareth as if He was alive and with them, though unseen. They were not recalling a memory which was growing dimmer as the days passed. They were worshipping a Person more real to them than were their earthly companions. Strange—this! Could there be anything in it? Perish the thought! No, no! A thousand times, no! He would stamp it out, crush it, finish it once and for all.

And then it happened—when least he expected it. He saw the Lord. At least, he saw a dazzling, blinding light. And he heard a voice, calling him by his name—"Saul, Saul". And a question: "Why are you persecuting *Me*?" "But I am not, Lord: I am persecuting Your followers." "It comes to the same thing; persecute the Body and you persecute the Head"—was this the beginning of St. Paul's doctrine of the Church? "Lord, Master, what do You want me to do?" You can theorise about this conversion experience; you can "explain" it in modern psychological terms; if you are silly, you can think you have rationalised it by talking about the experiences of epileptics. What is sheer sober fact is this—that what happened on the Damascus Road that day, followed by the ministrations of Ananias and the baptism of Saul (Acts 9, 10–19), gave birth to one whose achievement, according to so prejudiced a critic as the late Lord Birkenhead, makes the work of Alexander the Great or Napoleon fade into insignificance.

St. Paul himself described what happened to him in a variety of ways in the letters which he later wrote. He said, for example, that he had been grasped by Christ (Philippians 3, 12), as if some mighty Hand had laid hold of him and turned him round in his tracks. He said that in his case creation had taken place all over again (II Corinthians 4, 6), darkness giving way to light and chaos to order at the divine *fiat* (clearly he had in mind the old Genesis story of creation). Whenever a man comes to be in Christ, there creation takes place over again (II Corinthians 5, 17), he added. He had received a revelation—there was no other word for it—"God was pleased to reveal His Son to him" (Galatians 1, 16): he was "set apart for the Gospel of God" as surely as his parents had thought him "set apart" for a life of Rabbinic devotion. He was a Pharisee indeed— but of a very different sort! (Romans 1, 1). His letters are bestrewn with references, sometimes direct, sometimes oblique, to the shattering event which happened to him on the Damascus Road and which altered the whole pattern of his life and thought and writings.

It is this event, I believe, and the life of happy slavery and discipleship which followed it, which gives the clue to the writings of the apostle. They cannot be understood without some understanding of the man and his conversion, nor, I believe, can they be *fully* understood without some kind of entry into fellow-discipleship, however that entry comes. For St. Paul was not primarily a theologian or philosopher. He was primarily a disciple, a willing slave of Jesus, and an evangelist and pastor of those for whom he believed his Lord had died and risen. Put it another way and we may say that we shall only understand the terms which we most naturally associate with St. Paul—justification, sanctification, redemption, and so on—when we have entered into the meaning of the experience which underlies and undergirds them all, namely, the fundamental experience of being "in Christ". Those two monosyllables, which occur again and again in the Pauline writings, are the most crucial key to the understanding of the man, of his thinking, of his writing, and of his influence down the centuries and throughout the world.

To be "in Christ" was to leave behind for ever the world in which a man sought to achieve his spiritual goal by self-effort or by good works. It was to enter a world in which it was patently clear that *no* righteousness could be achieved that way. When a man is found to be "in Christ", his status of being right with God (than which there can be no more important thing in this world or the next) is seen to be based, not on law, but on reliance on Christ (Philippians 3, 9). That is to say, he ceases to attempt to build up a credit account of good works with God, so that at the last day the scales of his good and bad works may *at least* balance! He sees, once the scales are off his eyes and he is baptised into the family of God (Acts 9, 18), that he is one of this community of the new-born not by reason of what he has done or achieved, but by the sheer mercy and grace of God in Christ. He has no righteousness of his own—nor ever will have. All he can bring to his redemption is the sin from which to be redeemed; and the miracle is that God accepts those dirty rags and clothes him in spotless garments. It was this insight—this revelation—which separated him for ever from his old religion; and, let it be

18

added, which separates the true Christianity from the false to-day. A nation of shopkeepers like ourselves naturally thinks in terms of *doing* rather than *being*. It takes a revelation to see that God does not deal with us on a business basis at all, but according to His mercy incorporates us into Christ. Then it is that we look up to God as Jesus in the days of His flesh looked up, and cry out, using the very word that He did, "Abba! Father!", the Spirit bearing witness with our spirit that we are children of God, and if children, then heirs of God and fellow-heirs with Christ (Romans, 8, 15-17).

Of this profound, sensational discovery the Epistles of St. Paul are full. There is a jubilation about this religion of the apostle which has an authentic ring. "Justified"—he uses a forensic word to help him to get across a mighty act of God and an unspeakable experience—"justified by faith, we have peace with God through our Lord Jesus Christ" (Romans 5, 1). But there is more to it than that. When this takes place within a man, powers become operative in him of which he knew nothing before. The seventh chapter of the Epistle to the Romans is a famous chapter in which St. Paul describes the miserable state of the man who knows the right, but has no power to carry it into effect. It is, indeed, an elaboration of Ovid's well-known words, "I see the better and approve it. I do the worse." "So I find it to be a law that when I want to do right, evil lies close at hand. For I delight in the law of God, in my inmost self, but I see in my members another law at war with the law of my mind and making me captive to the law of sin which dwells in my members. Wretched man that I am! Who will deliver me from this body of death?" The first person pronoun occurs very frequently in this chapter. Who is this "I"? No doubt it is far more than Saul of Tarsus. It is a generic term. It is unregenerate mankind. But it *is* Saul of Tarsus. It *is* autobiographical. The "lusty little boy" (as C. H. Dodd describes him) who "was once alive apart from the law" and then woke up to find that he had transgressed the commandment and was in an appalling mess (7, 9–11) was indeed a lad who lived at Tarsus in an orthodox Jewish home. And the dilemma in which he found himself persisted through adolescence into young manhood. Wretched man, indeed! Was there any way out? There was. The next chapter, that great eighth chapter which has been called "the Gospel of the Holy Spirit" expounds the way of release. There is a new principle at work in those who are "in Christ Jesus". There are the energies of the Holy Spirit who dwells in the child of God, that very Spirit who was operative in raising Jesus from the dead and who leads the sons of God through suffering to glory (vv. 11–17).

Nor is this experience of justification, of being redeemed (the phrase was commonly used in the first century of "buying out" slaves into freedom), one which can be understood in solitary terms. To be "in Christ" is to be in the community of the redeemed, in the fellowship of the Holy Spirit, in the Body of Christ. St. Paul is strong on his corporate metaphors because he has a mighty belief in the Church. He may describe it as a building (for example in Ephesians 2, 19–22) or as a body (for example in Ephesians 4, cp. Romans 12 and I Corinthians 12), or as a household (Ephesians 2, 19 cp. Galatians 6, 10) or as the new Israel of God (Galatians 6, 16); but all the terms are corporate in their significance. You cannot enjoy God in a corner all by yourself. You cannot say that you like Jesus but you don't like the Church. This great mystery (Ephesians 5, 32) is composed of those who are *simul justi et peccatores*, else you or I would not be in it. To be baptised into Christ is to be baptised into His body, that body which Christ loved and for which He gave Himself up.

I have barely touched on the great themes with which

St. Paul deals in his correspondence. I have left entirely untouched many of the things which he elaborates in his letters, sometimes in response to questions raised by his converts, sometimes in response to his own "intuition" that it is just *this* that they need if they are to be strong in Christ Jesus. But I have suggested that the *fons et origo* of his mighty religion was the experience of being "delivered from the dominion of darkness and transferred to the kingdom of God's beloved Son" (Colossians 1, 13), of being "in Christ", which came to him on the Damascus Road and when he was filled with the Spirit and baptised into Christ (Acts 9, 1-19).

Did time allow, it would be possible to run over the centuries illustrating the thesis that "whenever Christianity has been at its best, it has always been a Christianity which found in Pauline doctrine the real illumination of that which it believed" (A. W. F. Blunt: *The Epistle of Paul to the Galatians*, p. 30). I would myself put it more strongly than that. I would say that whenever there has been a renewed grasp of the truths at the heart of St. Paul's gospel, then there has been a revival of true religion. I would illustrate, for example, from St. Augustine in the fourth century who, young, brilliant and dissolute, let his eye fall on Romans 13, "Let us walk honestly, as in the day; not in rioting and drunkenness, not in chambering and wantonness; but put ye on the Lord Jesus Christ", and became one of the greatest figures of all the centuries of the Church's life. I would illustrate again from John Colet who, returning from Italy just before the fifteenth century merged into the sixteenth, announced a series of lectures on St. Paul's Epistles beginning with his Letter to the Romans. The effect of those lectures was as if a fire had been lit at which doctors and abbots, men of all ranks and titles, university students warmed their hands. It was as if a hammer were breaking up the cold scholasticism which hitherto had reigned in the Universities. I would illustrate from Martin Luther studying the Epistle to the Galatians in his cell, from Wesley with his 'heart strangely warmed' as he listened to Luther's commentary on that same Epistle, from Shaftesbury drawing all the heat of his passion for social reform from the fire of the word of God as he found it in the pages of Holy Scripture, not least in St. Paul. And so on and so on into our own times when the power of the Church's resistance against Nazis and in Africa against the Mau Mau movement drew much of its force from the inspiration of St. Paul's writings.

And if you were to ask me why I believed that history pointed this lesson so clearly, my reply would be that I believe St. Paul was the greatest exponent of the mind of Christ who ever lived. His language differed very greatly from that of his Master, but his great doctrines were derived from Him. There lay his secret, and there it still lies for you to rediscover, if you will.

II

ST. LUKE

WHAT do you make of the four Gospels? It would be easy to answer that they are four biographies of Jesus—*the* four biographies authorised by the Church. But it would be equally easy to reply that "biographies" is almost the last word which can be applied to them. Indeed, for all the "Lives of Jesus" which clutter up our shelves, it may be questioned whether it is possible to write a biography of Jesus at all. It was, I think, F. C. Burkitt who pointed out that within the pages of the Gospels, there are only about forty separate days within the life of Jesus of which we have any particular details at all! This is thin material from which to construct a life! Or again, consider the proportions of the Gospels, and in particular the amount of space given to the last week. Something like one-half to one-third of each Gospel is given to the events which led up to Good Friday and Easter Day. This is scarcely biography as we know it. It is, I think, deeply significant that the early Church attached so much importance to the Death and Resurrection of the Lord. Its members were conscious that (if I may misquote) "never man died like this Man"—that there was a meaning attaching to that great and victorious struggle with the powers of sin and death which has attached to no other death in the long aeons of history. Indeed in one of the earliest statements of the content of the primitive preaching, we see the same emphasis. "I declared unto you in the forefront of my message that which I also received," wrote

St. Paul in the fifties of the first century, "namely"—and the tone of the statement sounds like a very early Christian creed—"that Christ died for our sins . . . that He was buried, that He was raised, that He was seen" (I Corinthians 15, 3 ff.). Such disproportion, if we may use that word of four carefully planned books, may be doctrinally significant, but it militates against any description of the Gospels as *biographies*.

What, then, *are* the Gospels? We shall find an answer more nearly if we use the words "preaching material" and "apologetic" than if we use the word "biography". The story of a crucified Messiah was to the Jews a thing to stumble over, and to the Gentiles a good joke (I Corinthians 1, 23). The Jews wanted and longed for a Messiah with a mighty army at his heels, able and eager to drive the hated Romans into the sea. But He came to earth "a little baby thing, that made a woman cry". The Greeks wanted an addition to human knowledge, an antidote to ignorance, not a cathartic for sin. How preach the Christian message in a situation like that? *That* is the question which gave birth to the Gospels. John Mark, in the middle sixties at Rome, faced some such question. The voices of Peter and Paul had been silenced by the persecution of Nero, and every member of the catacomb church must have wondered if his turn was coming next. Should not the story of the early days, which Peter had told over and over again with almost monotonous repetitiveness, be put into writing? Hence that series of vivid colour snapshots which forms so large a part of the earliest of our four Gospels. A Rabbi turned Christian who has come down to history under the name of Matthew faced some such questions. What was the relation of Christianity to Judaism? Was it a legitimate or an illegitimate growth? Could Christianity be viewed as the full-blown flower of which Judaism had been the bud? The writer of the first Gospel believed it could only be understood in this way, and devoted his twenty-eight chapters, touched as they are with purple and gold, to prove the thesis. St. John cannot be classed as biography any more than St. Mark or St. Matthew—indeed it is less of a biography than either. Consider the silences—no story of the birth of Jesus, no story of His baptism, nor of His temptation, nor of His transfiguration, nor of the Institution of the Eucharist—and the list could be continued almost indefinitely. But preaching material—yes! And apologetic—certainly! And—I would add—*corrective*. But more of that in the next chapter.

Now what about *St. Luke*? Let us have a look at his two-volume work—the Gospel that goes by his name and that wonderful but ill-named book, *The Acts of the Apostles*. I am not going to worry you with a discussion of the authorship of the two books, whether they are in whole the work of one hand. There have been those who have doubted this. It shall suffice to quote you the words of one of the most recent commentators on *The Acts*, C. S. C. Williams (Fellow of Merton College, Oxford). He is alluding to those parts of *The Acts* which are written in the first person plural—"It is . . . extremely probable that the author of the we-sections wrote the rest of Acts and the Third Gospel." He bases his conclusion mainly on stylistic and linguistic arguments; and that will do for our purpose.

What have we got, then, in this very considerable body of material, fifty-two chapters in all? We certainly have a work of great beauty—Renan called the Gospel "the most beautiful book in the world", and he was not far out. There is a tradition, which goes back at least to the eighth century, that St. Luke was an artist. Certainly the man whom St. Paul called "dear Dr. Luke" (Colossians 4, 14) was a man of very considerable culture. You have only to compare his Gospel with that of St. Mark to see how he smoothes the grammatical and syntactical crudities of the latter; and you have only got to read the four verses which constitute his preface to Volume I to realise that he knows how to handle the medium of language. He has an almost uncanny way of conveying the "atmosphere" of the place in which his particular story is set. The tone, for example, of the opening chapters of the Gospel is Jewish through and through—the whole thing smacks of Judaism, Temple, sacrifices, priests, incense, worshippers, and what have you. But, as you read on and dip into Volume II, you are skilfully transported, as by a literary magic carpet, to a totally different world in which wandering Jews rub shoulders with Roman officials, and the mailed hand of Rome is seen to be maintaining that *pacis Romanae immensa majestas* of which Pliny wrote in a memorable phrase. Perhaps his medical training helped to make Luke as observant as he obviously was. The man of science (if that is not too modern a word to apply to this first-century doctor) was also a man of letters—if you do not feel almost seasick after reading the story of the shipwreck in Acts 27 you must either have an iron stomach or else a feeble imagination; anyhow, you are to blame, not St. Luke!

If those commentators are right who argue that St. Luke wrote for the "upper ten" of Graeco-Roman society, we may count it a fortunate thing that Christianity numbered among its early Gentile converts so cultured a person as he. I will not delay you to propound this case—I will only draw your attention to the fact that *The New English Bible New Testament* describes Theophilus, to whom both books are dedicated, as "your Excellency" (St. Luke 1, 3). That makes things pretty clear, even if you cannot follow B.H. Streeter (*The Four Gospels*, pp. 534 ff.) in identifying Theophilus (which means "God-lover") with Flavius Clemens, first cousin of the Emperor Domitian—a fascinating "scientific guess", if nothing more! Here, at least, is a cultured Gentile writer putting forth his two volumes to commend the faith to his fellow-Gentiles who would appreciate a good literary work when they saw it. It is *apologia* which needed no apology!

Now, you don't have to read *Acts* very carefully before you discover that St. Luke was a hero-worshipper of St. Paul. I used a little earlier the words "ill-named" when I referred to *The Acts of the Apostles*. St. Luke's second volume, whatever else it is, is certainly not that. Most of the Apostles *exeunt in mysterium*, so far as he is concerned. The two figures who loom up clear and masterful are Peter (who occupies our attention in the opening chapters) and Paul who dominates the stage from Chapter 9 to the end. There are plenty of other characters, some of them very colourful people like Stephen and Philip, but it is for those two above all others that St. Luke has eyes. Nor is it to be wondered at that St. Paul is his hero. The two men travelled together, I suppose by boat, by horse and by shanks' pony. You get to know a man pretty well like that. And when you treat him professionally, and bind his wounds, and heal his ague, and when you explain to him how the body works and he stops you in the middle of your treatment and starts expounding to you how the doctrine of the Body of Christ works — well, that's another story. Re-read those we-sections of the Acts — bits of travel-diary as they undoubtedly are (Acts 16, 10-17; 20, 5-21, 18; 27, 1-28, 16) and you will not need a great deal of imagination to see the inter-play of two fine minds and the fusing of two great spirits. "Dear Dr. Luke". "Dear Master Paul".

Let us have a look at those three passages in *Acts* in which St. Luke gives us his first-hand story of travel in company with his hero.

(i) Acts 16, 10-17. Here the two men are at Philippi. It was a place of considerable importance, having been founded by Philip of Macedon, father of Alexander the

Great, and conquered by the Romans in 168 B.C. In 31, Octavian had re-founded it, and it became a Roman colony with all the rights and privileges, including exemption from tribute, which that carried with it. It has been called "a little Rome away from Rome" and its inhabitants were immensely proud of their status. No doubt St. Paul, as a Roman citizen himself, felt thoroughly at home there. There was also a small Jewish settlement there. The town was on a great East-West highway. Everything pointed to its importance as a place in which to plant the Gospel. It was to the Philippians that St. Paul sent the happiest of his letters.

It does not require a great stretch of imagination to envisage the two men, apostle and doctor, at work in that place. The apostle is "at home" in his Jewish and Roman contacts. The doctor, Gentile that he is, finds much that is congenial to his taste. What are they talking about? The weather? The history of the place? No doubt. But even more certainly, the establishment of the reign of King Jesus, that greater monarch than the Caesar on his throne, in that very city. A church is founded there, right in "the leading city of the district of Macedonia and a Roman colony" (v. 12). Philippi is no longer only an outpost of Rome; it is an outpost of the Kingdom of heaven.

(ii) Acts 20, 5-21, 18. This second we-passage gives us the story of the two men leaving Philippi, the tragi-comic tale of Eutychus falling out of the window asleep while St. Paul preached (surely the only man who ever managed to sleep during that exciting performance!), and then the journey to Miletus. This last is important, because Miletus was the port of Ephesus, and Ephesus was the chief city of the Province of Asia. To Miletus, St. Paul summoned the elders of the Church at Ephesus, and gave them the most solemn charge which occupies the second half of Acts 20. Why does St. Luke devote so much space and give such care to this? The reason is obvious. He sees, as St. Paul saw, the crucial importance of getting the kingship of Jesus firmly planted there. St. Paul had spent longer at Ephesus than in any one other place, partly because he saw its strategic importance in the over all plan of evangelism in the Roman Empire; and partly because Ephesus was the centre of so many pagan faiths and heathen philosophies that the new faith of Christ would have much to contend with in the early years of its growth. The second half of Acts 20 is partly retrospective, partly hortatory, partly commendatory. It is a solemn document, precisely because so much hung on the establishment there, in the chief city of Asia, of the Kingdom of heaven.

The first half of chapter 21 tells the story of the journey of the two men from Miletus to Jerusalem, not without delay at Caesarea at the house of Philip the Evangelist, who had four unmarried daughters. (Dear Dr. Luke, I think you had a sense of humour; and were you a bachelor? If not, where was Mrs. Luke?). Warned by the prophet Agabus that if he went to Jerusalem he would run straight into trouble, St. Paul remains undaunted —he is ready "not only to be imprisoned but even to die at Jerusalem for the name of the Lord Jesus" (v. 13). He was a man with the keenest sense of strategy. Philippi, a little Rome away from Rome; Ephesus, the chief city of the Province of Asia; Jerusalem, the mother city of Judaism —the apostle and doctor talked them all over and determined that, come what may, they would, so far as in them lay, see to it that the Kingdom of God was preached there, and its implications understood (see especially 21, 17 ff.).

(iii) Acts 27, 1–28, 16. This, the last of the travel documents of St. Luke, gives us not only the story of the shipwreck but also —and much more important —the arrival of St. Paul and of his gospel in Rome. Here is climax indeed, superb climax. The news of the Kingdom has reached the heart of the Empire. It is, according to the all too familiar pattern, rejected by the Jews. St. Paul turns to the Gentiles—"they will listen" (v. 28). Volume II ends with the jubilant picture of the apostle "preaching the Kingdom of God and teaching about the Lord Jesus Christ quite openly and unhindered" (v. 31). The Kingdom of God has invaded the Kingdom of Caesar right at its centre. There is dramatic climax if ever there was such a thing. And they have done it together, apostle and doctor in harness! *Laus Deo*.

Now you will have noticed that, in our examination of these bits of travel-diary, I have made much of the idea of the preaching and planting of the *Kingdom* in four strategic centres (Philippi, Ephesus, Jerusalem, and Rome). I now wish to point out a phenomenon which may strike you as somewhat strange. This phrase, "the Kingdom", "the realm", of God, so central to the teaching of Jesus, is surprisingly sparse in its occurrence in St. Paul's Epistles. Once in the great Epistle to the Romans, once each in Galatians, Ephesians and I and II Thessalonians, twice in Colossians, five times in I Corinthians, never in II Corinthians—this gives some idea of how thinly the phrase is spread over the considerable range of St. Paul's writings. Now I believe that the apostle has other ways of getting the *idea* across—that is another story. But the *phrase* he generally avoids. Why? The reason is not, I think, far to seek. His writings were designed for *general* reading in the Christian congregations. They were in no sense exclusive. They might be picked up and read anywhere at any time, and no doubt copies were made and passed on from church to church. If, in *such* documents, the major theme had been clothed in language about a Kingdom belonging to one, the Lord Jesus, that would have been to wave a red rag in the face of the Roman bull. No doubt the Kingdom of God and the kingdom of Caesar would have to clash. But nothing was to be gained by precipitating a head-on collision before the time. Let the phrase "the Kingdom of God" (or "of heaven", or "of Jesus") be played very lightly in any specifically Christian literature that could in any sense be called popular. That did not involve disloyalty to the central teaching of the Christian Faith. It was simply the course of wisdom to be pursued by those whose Master had taught them to be "wise as serpents and harmless as doves".

So much for the apostle. When we come to his companion, the doctor, the situation is quite different. "His theme" (writes A. R. C. Leaney, *A Commentary on the Gospel according to St. Luke* (1958) p. 34) "was the reign of Christ, how it is established, how it must be maintained." This I shall elaborate in a moment. Now I would make the point that this is precisely the theme, above all others, that he must get across when we remember the particular class of people whom he is trying to reach with his message. "His Excellency", Theophilus, must see what is involved in the rise of this movement, in its spread across the breadth of the Empire, and in its firm planting in the very centre of Rome itself. Christ and Caesar are face to face. Love and force look each other in the eye. Which would endure? History would declare. St. Paul, writing for the common man, might soft-pedal in his use of language; St. Luke, writing for the 'upper ten', must make the issue unmistakably clear.

How does St. Luke tackle his theme, the reign of Christ? He does it with supreme skill. The dullest of his readers could not get away with the idea that, because the Christian movement sprang from Jewish soil, it was confined in its scope to Jews. Luke's genealogy of Jesus goes back to Adam, the head of the human race (3, 38), unlike Matthew's which goes back to Abraham (1, 2). Simeon, devout Jew that he is, perceives that the Infant Christ is to be "a light

31

for revelation to the *Gentiles*", as well as "for glory to thy people Israel". "All flesh" — St. Luke quotes the passage from Isaiah with obvious delight — "all flesh will see the salvation of God" (3, 6). The first sermon that Jesus preached after His baptism was designed to show that God was confined within the bounds of no narrow nationalism (4, 25–27). Jesus finds a greater faith in a Roman officer than He found in any Israelite (7, 9); and teaches, to the great discomfort of the orthodox, that there will be folk from the far quarters of the earth sitting down at table in the kingdom of God and the Jews themselves shut out (13, 28–30). Repentance and forgiveness of sins are to be preached *to all nations* (24, 47). St. Luke's universalism is plain for all to see on page after page of his Gospel.

Against that background of universalism, St. Luke presents the Figure of Christ the King, and "the series of events by which He claimed His throne" (Leaney, op. cit. p. 34). "Of His *Kingdom* there will be no end," says the angel to Mary (1, 33). "I must preach the good news of the *Kingdom of God*," Jesus says (4, 43) — St. Mark in the parallel passage simply says "preach". He enters Jerusalem at the end of His ministry, as a *King*, and refuses to rebuke those who hail Him as such with the words "Blessed be the King who comes" (19, 38–40). And, as near the end of His earthly ministry He sits at table with His followers, He assigns to them, as His Father assigned to Him, a *Kingdom* (22, 29). St. Luke "is . . . governed by the idea of the Kingdom and its association with the supper — both the banquet to come and the present supper which fore-shadows it: he links the actions and sayings in the upper room with the Kingdom which he expects. It is not a covenant which the Lord inaugurates, but a kingdom" (Leaney, op. cit. p. 74). Indeed, the *death* of Jesus is to St. Luke not something which is done by superior forces to one who is powerless to oppose them. On the contrary,

He, Jesus, is the great actor in the chain of events which culminated in the resurrection. He—mark the strange and majestic phrase—"fulfils His exodus at Jerusalem" (9, 31), i.e. He does in royal power what Moses had prefigured, defeats man's foes of sin and death, and brings them into the Promised Land of deliverance. So St. Luke "sets Jesus not on the throne of Israel only, but also on the throne of the universe". The royal progress reveals the effect which the King has upon those among whom He moves. "He makes His way through angry crowds without harm, He excites the awe of His followers, He raises the dead, heals, and forgives . . . is greater than Solomon, greater, it is hinted, than Elijah", and so on (Leaney, op. cit. pp. 34–5).

This, in brief, is the Christ of the Gospel according to St. Luke, the Christ as seen by one who himself was a Gentile convert, and a friend of that apostle of the hospitable mind who, himself a citizen of Rome and proud of it, was even prouder of being a citizen of the Kingdom of heaven. Volume II of St. Luke's great work is a study in how that Kingdom fared in its first encounter with the Roman Empire. The subsequent chapters of Church History have continued the tale—up to our own day. The most exciting chapter of that tale has been written, and is being written, in the story of the last century and a half or two centuries, in the expansion of the Church throughout the world. The end is not yet. But the Christian conviction holds that the day will dawn when "the kingdoms of this world shall indeed become the kingdom of our God and of His Christ". Meanwhile the Christian is, like St. Paul, put in trust with the Good News of the Kingdom, the Reign of Christ, and committed, by his baptism and by his committal to Christ, to its extension and its furtherance.

III

ST. JOHN

AT the beginning of the last chapter, I suggested that the Synoptic Gospels cannot be classed as biography, in the sense in which we moderns understand the term. I went on to say that I thought St. John was even less of a biography of Jesus than the first three Gospels. I drew your attention, in passing, to the extraordinary omissions in the Fourth Gospel which must strike any intelligent reader very forcibly—no story of the birth, baptism, temptation, or transfiguration of Jesus, nor of the institution of the Eucharist, and so on. I suggested that what we *have* got in the Fourth Gospel is preaching material, apologetic, and *corrective*.

If—as I think we may—we follow the almost unanimous tradition of the Church and place the writing of the Fourth Gospel in the city of Ephesus, in the Province of Asia, we shall, I think, get a good deal of light on the book. If, further, we place it round about the turn of the first century, we shall receive further light. Both place and date are highly significant. A glance at a map will show that Ephesus, "the first city of Asia", stood on a main East to West trade-route. It was thus open not only to traffic in material goods, but to the traffic of ideas of all kinds. It was, as St. Paul had found out to his cost a generation or more previously, the great centre of the worship of the many-breasted goddess Diana. It was the Mecca of all kinds of cults and esoteric societies, an hospitable centre for the latest fashions in philosophy or new thought. Jew and

Gentile rubbed shoulders here; Christian and pagan mixed in market and home, in university and commerce. How should Christianity present itself in such a hurly-burly of ideas and theories as obtained in Ephesus? The question pressed for an answer with a particular urgency at the turn of the century. The problems of Christian origins— "What did Jesus *teach* about this? What did He *do* about that"?—were answered half a century earlier by reference to His disciples who had companied with Him on earth. Peter would say, "I remember . . ."; Mark would add, "I overheard Him say . . ." But now hardly a soul remained who had known Him in the flesh. It was a period fraught with very great danger for the Christian community. How far, and in what ways, should the Church adapt itself to modern conditions? How far should she interpret her message into terms current in Asia Minor seventy years after her Master had first appeared in Palestine? To what extent, indeed, need she hold at all to the "old paths"? Or, to change the metaphor, could she slip her moorings altogether and launch out into the open sea, forgetting that she had a Palestinian anchor?

We do not know what the answer to these questions might have been had there not lived at Ephesus, in the late nineties, one who was supremely well fitted to meet the particular problems of the Church of his day. I do not propose to argue, at this point, the knotty problem of the authorship of the Fourth Gospel. It is a question which the examiners are very fond of setting, a problem over which floods of critical ink have been spilt. Should I be considered a heretic of the highest rank if I said that I thought it one of the questions of *least* importance in a Gospel which bristles with problems of great importance? I would make only two remarks about this controversial subject. The first is to draw the attention of anyone interested in the subject to a too little-known book of Bishop A. C. Headlam's,

The Fourth Gospel as History, published posthumously in 1948 —a book very incisive in its pungent criticisms of certain woolly-headed critics. The second remark is to remind you of some powerful words of the late Sir Edwyn Hoskyns. He writes of the author of the Fourth Gospel that "he has, in fact, so burnt himself out of his book that we cannot be certain that we have anywhere located him as a clear, intelligible figure in history. At the end of our inquiry he remains no more than a voice bearing witness to the glory of God. So anonymous is his book, so intentionally anonymous, that there is in it, apart from the shy little '*I suppose*' of the last verse, no 'ego' except the 'Ego' of Jesus, the Son of God. The author of the book has effaced himself, or rather, has been decreased and sacrificed, in order that the truth may be made known and in order that the Eternal Life which is in God may be declared". (*The Fourth Gospel*, p. 5.)

But of this it seems to me we may be reasonably certain —that, whether we hold to direct Apostolic authorship, or whether, with Archbishop Bernard, we hold the view that the Apostle was "behind" the writing of the Gospel rather as Peter was behind Mark, we have in this Gospel "an interpretative expression of a memory". That phrase is Archbishop Temple's, and it is one worth pondering. Memory and interpretation combine, and who is to divide the seamless robe which is the result? Who is to say with any element of nice precision, "*this* is memory, and *that* is interpretation"? As well might one seek, by letting down a bucket at the confluence of two rivers, to draw up a bucketful of this or that! Wordsworth, who had the singular good sense to go not only to the right University, but to the right College in that University, wrote, you may remember, in *The Prelude*, of his thoughts many years later about his undergraduate days at St. John's, Cambridge:

> "I cannot say what portion is in truth
> The naked recollection of that time,
> And what may rather have been called to life
> By after-meditation."

Just so. Naked recollection; after-meditation; and the play of the Spirit of God, over the space of a couple of generations, on a mind singularly fertile and a spirit singularly devout—*that* is behind what we know as the Fourth Gospel.

When we were planning the new buildings for the London College of Divinity which now stand at Northwood, we included at the East end of the Chapel a big circular window. As the College is dedicated to St. John the Evangelist, we arranged with the artist that the symbol of the eagle should occupy a prominent place in the window. For tradition has it that of all birds the eagle soars nearest to heaven while its penetrating gaze pierces shrewdly through the air to the earth. What better symbol for the Fourth Evangelist? Of all the four, it is he who soars highest in his doctrine. What other writer can touch that matchless prologue with its massive doctrine of the Word, Agent of Creation, for us men and for our salvation become flesh? He soars up to the very gates of heaven. And yet how almost brutally he holds us to a down-to-earth doctrine of the Incarnation. Bishop Launcelot Andrews, pondering on the phrase, "And the Word became flesh", says: "I add yet farther; what flesh? The flesh of an infant. What, *Verbum infans*, the Word an infant? The Word, and not able to speak a word? How evil agreeth this! This He put up . . . a stable for His palace, a manger for His cradle, poor clouts for His array." To this St. John held the Ephesian Church, interpreting the Gospel in terms which his Gentile contemporaries would understand, the while he held them immovably to the great events which had taken place at the beginning of the century in Palestine. He

37

anchored the Eternal in human history. He saw the Eternal God in One who was hungry, who wept, who was tired, who thirsted, who was indeed Very Man. In Jesus of Nazareth St. John saw the truth of what Goethe was to give expression to many centuries later: "The highest cannot be spoken; it can only be acted." Jesus was the divine compassion acted out on the stage of human history (It was Pavlova who, on being asked what she meant by a dance which she had just performed, replied: "Do you think I would have danced it if I could have said it?"). Jesus *is* what God has to say to men. Hitherto men had been bearers of the Word of God. Jesus *was* the Word of God. Hitherto the prophets had said: "Thus saith the Lord." But Jesus *was* God's Word in human flesh. *This* is the Christ of the Fourth Gospel.

I mentioned—just in passing—that St. John has no record of the Transfiguration, that event which in all three Synoptics occupies so important a place in the story of the breaking through of the divine glory so that the privileged few *saw*. The reason for this omission is, I think, two-fold. First, there was no need to re-tell the story which all three Synoptists had already written. Those Gospels were now more or less the common property of the Church. The Fourth Evangelist must restrict himself to a selection of incidents of especial significance for his own purpose, if the limits of an ancient book were not to be over-run. But the second reason for the omission of the story of the Transfiguration goes deeper than this—the whole Gospel is the story of the glory of God breaking through and seen in the Face of Jesus Christ. In fact, over the book might be inscribed, with great accuracy, the stanza from the *Te Deum*: "Thou art the King of Glory, O Christ; Thou art the everlasting Son of the Father." That would well epitomise the approach of the Fourth Evangelist to his august theme. Let me illustrate the point I am trying to make—and I must do so with some little care, for the concept of *glory* in St. John differs *toto caelo* from the idea of glory which commonly obtains in our own world-order.

We begin with the prologue, "The Word became flesh and 'tented' among us"—the very word "tented" speaks of the frailty of human nature, of a dwelling-place humble and temporary for Him who was with God and indeed was God. "The Word became flesh and 'tented' among us, and we beheld His—humiliation." So you or I would have completed the sentence. Not so St. John! "We beheld his *glory*!" If you want to see the glory of God, the Evangelist would say to us, you do not look for it in the usual paraphernalia of majesty, in the trappings of trumpets and angels and streets of gold. No! You find it in the humiliation of a manger and in the shame of a Cross. So did God stoop to conquer. This is a major theme in this book. Indeed one might almost say that it is *the* theme on which the Evangelist constructs a series of variations. Supremely at the Cross is the glory of God seen. There—at the place of humiliation and of self-emptying, there—at the place of which Cicero wrote, "far be the very name of the Cross not only from the body of Roman citizens but also from their thought, eyes and ears,"—*there*, where the Son of Man is "lifted up", is the glory of God to be seen. As a matter of fact, the use of the word "lift up" for "crucify"—a peculiarly Johannine use of the term—is more than spatial in its significance. Of course it *is* that. The victim of a Roman crucifixion was laid upon the wood flat on the ground; the nails were fastened; a hole was dug in the ground; and then the cross was jerked into position, with its human burden "lifted up" between earth and sky. But when the Fourth Evangelist speaks of "lifting up" the Son of Man he has more in mind than spatial elevation. There "placarded up" for all to see (if we may borrow a somewhat similar phrase from St. Paul in

Galatians 3, 1) was the divine love incarnate, drawing all men unto Him.

The classic passage which elaborates this theme is found in St. John 12. The record is given of certain Greeks coming to Philip with the request, "Sir, we would like to meet Jesus." So Philip of the Greek name comes to Andrew, also of the Greek name, and together they tell Jesus. In reply Jesus says jubilantly, "The hour has arrived that the Son of Man should be glorified." That is to say, this is the audience for whom the message of the Good News (not to say the Fourth Gospel itself) was intended. The scope of the influence of the Incarnation is as wide as the Love of God. But there is a sobering note which accompanies the jubilation of Jesus. "Glorified? Yes; but unless a corn of wheat falls into the ground and *dies* . . . Now is my soul storm-tossed; and what shall I say? Father, save me out of this hour? No; for this cause I came to this hour. Father, glorify Thy Person." *That*—precisely that— is the background (in vv. 20–27) of the famous sentence (v. 32): "I, if I be lifted up, will draw all men unto Me." And the Evangelist, lest we should make an error and think that Jesus was referring to the glory of the Ascension, added the comment (v. 33): "In saying this, He was signifying by what kind of death He would die." *This* is the Christ of the Fourth Gospel.

Or again, consider the foot-washing, that great opening section of the thirteenth chapter which in St. John takes the place which the institution of the Eucharist occupies in the Synoptics, and which is the writer's way of introducing the Passion story. We have only time to mention in passing the almost breath-taking contrasts which the Evangelist draws of the One who, having loved His own who were in the world, demonstrated His love for them to the limit (this is the right translation of 13, 1). On the one hand, He knew that the Father had given all things into

His hands, and that He had proceeded from God and was going to God—here is incarnate majesty. On the other hand, He laid aside His garments and, because the others were too pre-occupied with the question of their status in the little community to give a thought to the necessary "chores" which had to be done, HE took a towel, HE girded Himself, HE poured water into a basin, HE washed the disciples' feet. Without that cleansing, there could be no fellowship. The foot-washing symbolised the cleansing of the disciples effected by the Passion. There was only One who could bring that about. It is the Christ of the Fourth Gospel.

Now this section about the foot-washing, followed as it is by the story of Jesus' betrayal and the giving of the new commandment, serves as an introduction to the priceless long section of discourse (chs. 14–16) in which Jesus breaks the news to the disciples that He is about to leave them, but that they will not be bereft orphans; on the contrary He will come to them in the Person of His Other Self. He calls this Other Self by a title which never occurs in the first three Gospels—the Paraclete. Now it is not the function of this chapter to try to deal with the doctrine of the Holy Spirit as reflected in the Fourth Gospel—that is a story in itself! But in so far as Jesus implied in the phrase "another Paraclete" (chs. 14, 16) that He Himself had been a Paraclete to His followers, we must, in considering the Christ of the Fourth Gospel, seek to find some meaning in the term. What *is* a Paraclete? Here let me register a strong protest against the translation "Comforter". It is through Tyndale and Wycliffe that we trace that rendering, though it must be said in their favour that the stress in their day on the word comforter was on the idea of strengthening rather than of tear-drying (cf. *fortify*, *fortification*, etc.). The rendering *consolator*, which occurs in Hilary, Jerome and Orosius, is even less satisfactory. The root meaning of the word Paraclete is "to call alongside to one's help".

41

Now, when I ring up an A.A. man to come to the aid of the mechanically ignorant (that is me!) I want more than sympathy, more than the (metaphorical) drying of my tears. I want to be set going again; I want the power to *get there*! Now it would not be difficult to prove, if time did but allow, that in the pages of the New Testament the root idea behind Paraclete is the idea of *stimulation* and *inspiration* (cf. e.g. Acts 9, 31; Romans 12, 8; 15, 4–5; Hebrews 13, 22, etc.). This *is* the function of God the Holy Spirit— not simply to dry our tears (the Church is more than an ambulance unit to pick up the broken bits of society and comfort their troubles, though that is a very necessary function). It is His work to stab awake sleepy consciences, to set fire to woolly thinking, to initiate vigorous mental activity and ethical action; to—dare I say it with all reverence?—to stick a pin into the sluggishness of our thinking and the complacency of our living. "I believe in the Holy Ghost, the Lord, the Life-Giver", the Paraclete, the Stimulater. *Do* you? Well, the early Church did, because they had found that Jesus had been precisely that to them during His early Ministry, and what He had begun His Other Self continued. He took a little crowd of intellectually and spiritually lethargic men and women—people who, just like ourselves, loved to say, "It was good enough for Moses, so it is good enough for me—as it was in the beginning, is now, and ever shall be, world without end"—He took them and so shook them, so stimulated them, so made them re-think their whole attitude to God, to others, to themselves, to sin, to life, to death, that by the time He had finished with them (or should we say *begun* with them?) they out-lived, out-thought, and out-died their contemporaries. Jesus the Paraclete—*this* is the Christ of the Fourth Gospel.

Near the beginning of this chapter I described the Fourth Gospel as preaching material, as apologetic, as corrective.

Can you begin to see the significance of those terms? Imagine yourself a young Christian in Ephesus in A.D. 95. It is clear that the old Evangelist has not long to go. The Church will soon be bereft of her greatest figure, and her last link with the apostolic age will be broken. To some extent *you* must continue the work which he will so soon lay down. What shall you preach? MARK? No—for vivid as that was, it would do for the persecuted Roman Church of the sixties, but hardly for the intelligentsia of Ephesus a generation later. MATTHEW? Certainly not, for that massive book was meant almost exclusively for Jews, and you are surrounded by rather supercilious Gentiles. LUKE? Hardly, for here at the turn of the century you have run into a hornet's nest of problems which LUKE (for all its beauty) hardly begins to face. No; the new age is calling for a new interpretation of the old Gospel, and it is that which you have to hand in St. JOHN. Yes, it is the old Gospel, for the Evangelist allows of no loosening from the old Palestinian moorings. That Life, that Death and Resurrection, which took place when Pontius Pilate was governor of Judaea, root Christianity in history, and are part of its "given-ness". You cannot advance *from* that into a vague, airy-fairy "spiritual" religion. "The Word became flesh". "We handled: we saw: we bear witness" (I St. John 1, 1). In so far as the Church was beginning to shift from that, so far does the Fourth Gospel correct her. But it puts the central message, unchangeable in its given-ness and in its glory, in terms which the modern thinker can appreciate and understand. Its *apologia* is intelligent (which is more than can be said of much modern preaching, God forgive us!). Here is preaching material for the thinker of Ephesus, A.D. 100; here is *apologia* which can be understood by the people; here is *corrective* to influences which might have taken the "bite" from Christianity had not the mystic-theologian of Ephesus stopped the rot.

43

I cannot, however, end this chapter without one closing word, and that, as I believe, a word of paramount importance if we are to understand the Gospel and to glimpse the Christ whom it seeks to present to us. I should consider that this chapter had been a disastrous failure if I left you with the impression that the Fourth Evangelist was primarily a philosopher whose main task was to beat other Ephesian philosophers at their own game! It is abundantly clear that the writer was, above all things else, an evangelist whose one great passion was that men, on reading his book, should come face to face with Him of whom he wrote and bow themselves in total and unconditional surrender to His claims. That this was his avowed intent he declares at the conclusion of the main part of his book (20, 31 – chapter 21 is an epilogue). Let me quote his three-fold purpose in writing as he states it for us: "These things are written that you may believe (i) that Jesus is the Christ", that is to say, that the witness of the other Gospels *holds* as to the self-revelation of God in Jesus of Nazareth; (ii) that this Jesus is "the Son of God", that is to say, that the main structure of Christian theology which we associate with such names as St. Paul and St. Peter also holds. That, you might say, is the writing of a theologian-philosopher. But the writer does not stop there. He has a third purpose in writing. It is (iii) "that, believing, you may have life in His Person". Here is the *Evangelist* at work. He has known this Jesus down the long years. Life would not have been life without Him. The very meaning of life is in that "believing" of which he writes, that person to Person committal which re-makes men and women and lets loose in them powers of which heretofore they have not dreamed.

"My Lord and my God," said Thomas, when he saw the wound prints in the hands and side of the risen Lord. It is the avowed intent of the Evangelist that his readers should, one and all, come to that same conclusion.

44

IV

THE AUTHOR OF THE EPISTLE TO
THE HEBREWS

Most of us have stood, at one time or another, on the shore of some great ocean and watched the tide come in. It seemed as if the power of the universe lay behind those breakers, advancing with a kind of inexorable majesty. As we watched, we listened; and the sound of the breakers matched the sight that met our eyes. The thunder of the waves was offset by the sparkling of the sun on the spume.

I often think of a scene like that when I read the opening verses of the Epistle to the Hebrews, especially when I read them in the original. *Polumerōs kai polutropōs*—"at sundry times and in divers manners"—the Authorised Version catches something of the majesty of the theme which the writer is about to propound. He sets out that theme in 1, 1–4. It is no less a subject than the full revelation of God in the Person of His Son—an august subject indeed!

Sir Robert Falconer, in his little book *The Heart of the New Testament* (pp. 34–35), writes thus of the author of this Epistle: He "is a contemplative soul, looking away from the world of shadows to Jesus the Captain of all the faithful who has also brought the faith to completion. Philosophical, cultivated, pensive, he meditates on the Apostle and High Priest of the final religion. Worshipful, as a mediæval saint in a cathedral, he feels himself while still on earth carried far from the shadowy ritual of Israel to the throne of grace, where the perfect High Priest in the heavenly Sanctuary, touched with a feeling for human infirmities, is ever making intercession for us." That is well said: and to many of the ideas adumbrated by Sir Robert we shall return before long.

As in other chapters in this book, we shall leave the problems of authorship, destination and so forth barely touched on. This ground has been covered again and again in great detail, and any introduction to the New Testament will give the reader the necessary details. Suffice it to say that the book is anonymous. Both style and general approach combine to make it highly unlikely that St. Paul was the author; and we should probably do well to follow Origen's reserved caution when he said that God alone knows who wrote the book. But if we cannot put a name to the writer, we can conjure up in our mind's eye a pretty good picture of him. Nowhere in the New Testament is his literary style surpassed—here is obviously a man of very considerable culture. He is well read—and not only in the Old Testament. He knows his Philo, that strange Jewish figure who bridged the last century B.C. and the first century A.D. (his dates were about 20 B.C.–A.D. 50), and who sought to bridge the gulf that yawned between Greek and Jewish ways of thought and of religion. He knows his classical writers—his dictum about our Lord that "He learned obedience through the things He suffered" (5, 8) reminds us of *pathos mathos*, "suffering is education", in the Agamemnon. He knows how to use the method of allegorical interpretation of Old Testament scripture, a method which does not naturally appeal to us historically minded moderns—that is why we find the section, for example, on Melchisedek (chs. 7 ff.) difficult. But he is far more than a man of letters. He is a man who knows the way through into the Presence of God, who knows the meaning of worship, and who finds it supremely good.

So much, or rather so little, for the writer. What about the readers? The generally accepted view is that they were Jewish Christians—it is doubtful whether many Gentile Christians would have been sufficiently knowledgeable to appreciate the constant references, direct and indirect, to the Old Testament of which the Epistle is full. These Christians had not recently entered into their new life in Christ—by this time they ought to be teachers (5, 12) showing signs of maturity and advance in the faith. In the early days of their discipleship they had undergone persecution (10, 32–34), though this persecution had not been "to the point of shedding your blood" (12, 4). The tone of the Epistle suggests the likelihood of further persecution ahead—perhaps we can put the writing of it somewhere between Nero's persecution (he died in 68 A.D.) and Domitian's (he died in 96 A.D., and the persecutions took place towards the end of his reign).

What was the occasion of the writing of this "word of exhortation", as the writer describes his work in 13, 22? Perhaps this very description gives us the clue. It is an apt summary of what indeed is hardly a letter and much more a thesis or sermon. The element of *exhortation* is constant. We note how persistently the writer uses the words "Let us . . ." and "we ought . . ." (e.g. 2, 1; 4, 1, 11, 14, 16; 6, 1; 10, 22–25; 12, 1–2). It is clear that he is concerned about the spiritual welfare of Christians who show signs of immaturity, even of apostasy. So far from going on, they are slipping back; and the note of encouragement and exhortation is balanced by the sober note of grave warning (3, 12; 10, 26 etc.). Clearly all is not well. There are signs of great spiritual danger. And the writer, "philosophical, cultivated, pensive" as he undoubtedly is, has a heart sufficiently pastoral to warn his friends of their danger.

It is one thing to warn. It is another to suggest a remedy. Our writer does both. He has not the slightest atom of doubt as to the answer to apostasy, to retrogression, to spiritual immaturity. That answer may be summarised in the two words: "Consider Jesus" (3, 1; cp. 12, 3). Indeed, the whole of the Epistle to the Hebrews, might be called "A consideration of the Person of Jesus". When, in the closing chapter of this book, we come to the *Revelation*, we shall find ourselves faced with a writing almost entirely different from the Epistle to the Hebrews. The problems facing the readers of the *Revelation* are those of active and cruel persecution—the fires are ablaze, whereas in the Epistle to the Hebrews they are at the most underground. But one thing these two books have in common. The problems may be different, but the answer is the same. Christ Jesus Himself is the answer, alike to the problems of immaturity and retrogression, and to the problem of virulent persecution. The Seer begins his book with a brilliant picture of the Christ in glory (ch. 1). The writer of the Epistle to the Hebrews devotes almost his entire Epistle to the description of Christ as he sees Him, and of His complete adequacy for the needs of the readers of the book.

We must, therefore, devote some care to a study of the Person of Christ as He is depicted for us in the chapters of this book. The study will be by no means complete. It will be outlinear. But it may be hoped that it will be suggestive. I select six facets as they are given to us in these thirteen chapters:

(i) *Son of God.* In the second verse of this Epistle the writer confronts us with Jesus as Son of God, the One in whom, in a unique way, God has spoken to men. It is but a small step from these tremendous opening verses to the doctrine of Christ as the Word of God as it is given to us in the first chapter of St. John. How much is crammed into these four verses—Christ as the Word of God (though the actual *term* is not used here), the heir of the universe, the agent of creation, the effulgence of God's splendour and the stamp of His being, the sustainer of all things, the purger of sins, the One seated at the right hand of Majesty on high, raised far above the angelic hosts. Phrase is piled on phrase to introduce the theme of Christ's superiority to the angels, in as much as He is Son while they are servants of the Most High. This facet of the Person of Christ, so firmly delineated in Chapter 1, is reverted to at least seven times elsewhere in the Epistle. It is a dominant theme.

Oscar Cullmann, in his *The Christology of the New Testament* (pp. 303–4), points out that for Mark, faith in the "Son of God" is very important; but, following Jesus' own attitude, he speaks of it with a certain reticence. "Paul writes *Kyrios* (Lord) more often, although the idea of divine sonship has great significance for him also. Surprisingly, the designation is not mentioned at all in the Pastoral Epistles or in James or Peter. It occurs only once in Revelation (2, 18) and twice in Acts (9, 20; 13, 33). . . . The "Son of God" concept dominates the Christology of Hebrews all the more in contrast."

(ii) *Our Brother*. Against this majestic background, it is the more surprising to find our author elaborating the fact that this Jesus, Son of God, is our Brother! "He is not ashamed to call them brethren" (2, 11). He might well be ashamed, for we are sinful and He is sinless. But He is not ashamed. He was "made like His brethren in every respect" (2, 17), the only exception being sin. The passage where the "Brotherhood" of Jesus is worked out is 2, 10 to 3, 1. I include 3, 1 because in this context it is obvious that, when the writer speaks of "holy brethren", he means brothers in that family of God whose Eldest Brother is Christ!

It may well be a fact that the writer of the Epistle to the Hebrews knew of the incident recorded in the closing verses of St. Mark 3. The brethren and the mother of

Jesus "standing without", sent to Jesus, calling Him. The crowd told Jesus of their desire to see Him. "But He answered them, saying, 'Who is My mother, or My brethren?' And He looked round on them which sat about Him, and said, 'Behold My mother and My brethren! For whosoever shall do the will of God, the same is My brother, and My sister, and mother.'"

Faithful to that passage, or at least to the tradition lying behind it, our author works out his theme in Chapter 2, verse 10, to Chapter 3, verse 1. That is the key passage. But it is part of a bigger theme which we may well consider here. I do not think that in any New Testament document is the complete humanity of Jesus so clearly enunciated and so insistently taught as it is in the Epistle to the Hebrews. In the Gospels there is hardly a more vivid description of the Agony in Gethsemane than that which is given to us in Hebrews 5, 7: "In the days of His flesh, Jesus offered up prayers and supplications, with loud cries and tears, to Him who was able to save Him from death, and He was heard for His godly fear." Nor is there a clearer passage in the Gospels describing Jesus' growth in the learning of obedience than that daring and moving verse (5, 8): "He learned obedience through what He suffered." With this we may compare these passages: "Because He Himself has suffered and been tempted, He is able to help those who are tempted" (2, 18). "He was faithful to Him who appointed Him . . ." (3, 2). "We have not a high priest who is unable to sympathise with our weaknesses, but one who in every respect has been tempted as we are, yet without sinning" (4, 15). "Jesus . . . who for the joy that was set before Him endured the cross, despising the shame" (12, 2). He "endured from sinners such hostility against Himself" (12, 3).

Just as the writer of the Fourth Gospel balances his doctrine of the Son of God with the strong dogma of His humanity, so our writer holds in tension and in close juxta-position the mighty doctrines of the Son of God and the human Jesus who is not ashamed to call us His brethren. Oscar Cullman (op. cit. p. 93) sums it up well: "The author of Hebrews, as perhaps no other early Christian theologian, had the courage to speak of the man Jesus in shockingly human terms—although at the same time he emphasised perhaps more strongly than any other the deity of the Son."

It takes no great powers of imagination to see what this doctrine meant to the readers of this Epistle, subject as they were to all the subtle pressures of a society predominantly un-Christian and often anti-Christian. Jesus had trodden the way before them. He had been tempted and tried. He had been a learner in the hard school of discipleship. He had gone through Gethsemane. Now, in very truth, He *knows*, because He *knew*. He has carried up our manhood into Godhead. You can maintain the fight if you believe *that* about Him who is not ashamed to be called your brother.

This matter is of such importance that I venture to draw your attention to an important passage in Professor Herbert Butterfield's *Christianity and History* (p. 119):

"What I must not do . . . is to make God less than a person—hanging as a shapeless vapour or an indifferen-tiated ooze, which is what people seem to arrive at when they want to believe in Him without committing them-selves to anything. And nothing seems to me to be more absurd than the picture which seemed to exist at one time of God as a sort of urge within matter itself— gradually discovering Himself and coming to conscious-ness in the course of ages as man developed. If there were to be a revelation of God to man, only a human being more human than we are would give us a vision that we should be capable of comprehending—one whose humanity was genuine and authentic, whose flesh was real flesh, so that if you pricked it it would hurt and bleed—one who actually got tired at the end of a day. I personally would feel strongly that it must be a human being under our conditions—limited in his knowledge, so limited that even his consciousness of his mission only came gradually, in a groping way at first; so limited that even the temptations which he suffered must be regarded as having been real to him and not a mere shadow-show."

It is some such human being as Professor Butterfield here describes who is presented to us by the author of the Epistle to the Hebrews.

(iii) *Apostle*. In 3, 1 Jesus is called Apostle. That is an unusual designation for the One who made apostles. Indeed, I do not think there is any other New Testament passage in which He is given that title. But, of course, the idea of Jesus being the One sent by God to accomplish His great mission is a familiar one in the Gospels, and is particularly congenial to the author of the Fourth Gospel. Indeed, it is one of his main themes, and reaches the climax of its development in St. John 20, 21, when the risen Lord says to the disciples, "*As My Father hath sent Me* even so send I you." Thus, without actually using the word 'Apostle' of our Lord, the fourth Evangelist underlines His apostleship.

Now there were apostles *and* apostles! Judas was an apostle, but he betrayed his master. Peter was the first of the apostles, but he denied his Lord. Jesus, on the other hand, was an Apostle who proved, at every point, "faithful to Him Who appointed Him" (3, 2). This idea links up with that concept of complete obedience which we have already noticed in 5, 8, etc.

At this point we may notice the great stress laid by our author on the whole life and death of Jesus as the doing of the will of God—as total response to His demands. The classic passage is 10, 5 ff. The old order of ritual sacrifices, offered year in year out, day in day out in the Temple, is finished. One final sacrifice has been offered. "Here am I... I have come to do Thy will, O God" (5, 7). The life lived in complete obedience, the apostleship faithfully carried out, the life-blood offered to God—that is the sacrifice to which all other sacrifices looked forward; and it is "by that will we have been consecrated through the offering of the body of Jesus Christ once for all" (10, 10).

(iv) *High Priest.* The categories of priest and victim, of altar and animal sacrifice, of blood and fire are difficult for us moderns to understand. They seem remote from our ways of thinking, little more than vestiges from days long gone by. And yet the dominant concept which, perhaps above all other, our author is anxious to put before us, clearly and distinctly, is the concept of Jesus as our great High Priest. "The whole letter deals with Him in this role." (O. Cullmann, op. cit. p. 89.) We must, therefore, try to see what this concept of priesthood and sacrifice is about.

First, let us note that the writer is at pains to point us, not backwards but upwards. If indeed he looks back—and, as we have seen, his writing is full of Old Testament allusions and quotations—it is only in order to say to the reader: "*Now* I point you upwards to One in whom the old shadows are seen to be just that. Now you have the reality. And that reality means that the old order of constantly reiterated sacrifices is done with for ever. No more a hierarchy of high priests and priests, sinning mortals as they were. No more the sacrificing of dumb animals with a view to the removal of human contaminations. Let us face it frankly, they never could take away sins or give a man what he most longs for, a clear conscience." So A. C. Welch can write: "These offerings are meant to remove physical impurity. And the means of cleansing was physical and external like the impurity which required to be removed. . . . A man who touched a dead body became ceremonially unclean, but the act might have been wholly involuntary on his part. . . . These uncleannesses were committed . . . 'through inadvertence'. And it was to atone for these, and only for these, that the sin-offering was valid. Numbers 15, 22–31, definitely prescribes that, when the congregation or an individual in it has contracted uncleanness through inadvertence, a sin-offering must be provided in order to make the necessary atonement. But it further definitely orders that any man who sins . . . voluntarily and with the knowledge of what he has done, can find no means of atonement. In such a case that soul shall be cut off from among his people." (*The Psalter in Life, Worship and History*, pp. 108–9).

Now things are different. Once, once for all, there has happened that which makes us see that the old, elaborate ritual was but a temporary means of making men conscious of the holiness of God, of their sinfulness, and of the vital need of their appearing in the presence of God but of appearing *prepared*. But since the first Good Friday, the day on which the obedience of the life of Jesus reached its climax in the laying down of His life, all the old system is antiquated, gone, done with. In so far as it spoke the Mind of God, it is all summed up and consummated in the offering of the Body of Jesus once for all. "Ring out the old. Ring in the new".

Professor William Barclay, in his excellent commentary on our Epistle, points out that if a high priest is to be a bridge-builder between man and God (and that is essentially his function), "he must know man and God. He must be able to speak to God for men, and to speak to men for God" (p. 25). Already we have seen that Jesus is perfectly suited to this function in as much as, according to this Epistle, He is *both* Son of God *and* our Brother, the faithful Apostle. He has been here; and from His own experience, often bitter in the extreme, He knows the stresses and temptations of His brethren. But He has not only been here. He is *now there* —"He ever lives to make intercession for us" (7, 25). The Christ of this Epistle is pre-eminently the Ascended Christ. The Ascension may be said to be the vantage-point of this letter, whereas the Resurrection is predominantly the vantage-point of St. Paul's letters. There at the right hand of the Majesty on high (1, 3) He sits, His sacrificial work accomplished, but His intercessory and representative work ever going on. H. B. Swete puts the thought of the Epistle well: "Our hope does not rest on a dead Christ, but on one who is *alive for evermore*; nor again on a Christ who merely lives, but on one who lives and reigns with God; nor, once more, simply on the fact of His exaltation, but on the knowledge that this exalted Person uses His opportunity to lay our case before God" (*The Ascended Christ*, p. 94). Swete goes on to point out that "the intercession of the Ascended Christ is not a prayer, but a life" (p. 95) —what He *is* in the perfection of His divine-human nature, in His capacity as "a throned Priest-King", constitutes His "effectiveness", if we dare use such a term. He has "passed through" (4, 14) the heavenly precincts into the presence-chamber of God. So we may with confidence *draw near* to the throne of Grace (4, 16).

It is in this context of ideas that religion is seen by our author as *worship*, as drawing near to God, as entrance into His holy presence. The sense of the awesome, of the numinous, is strong in this book. Herein lies one of its most important lessons for us sons and daughters of the twentieth century. For too many of us, worship is an optional extra for those who are "made that way". For a devout Hebrew, it was *the* matter of supreme importance. The primary question of life was: How, and on what conditions, may a man come into the presence of Almighty God? Indeed, it would not be too much to say that the whole weighty sacrificial system was an attempt to answer precisely that question. The burden of our great Epistle is to say to all men: There is a way through. Jesus is that way. He has offered up —not some animal sacrifice but —Himself (7, 27). He has done it once for all (7, 27; 9, 12; 10, 10). *He ever lives.* That means, in the words of Binney, that

> "There is a way for man to rise
>   To that sublime abode,
>   An offering and a sacrifice,
>   A Holy Spirit's energies,
>   An Advocate with God".

(v) *Pioneer.* There is so much else in this Epistle which ought to be said about Christ as High Priest, but to say more would be to make the section over-long. However, it will already have been seen that our divisions are somewhat artificial —each flows into the other. Because He is Son of God and Very Man, He can be our great High Priest. So this leads on to an unusual word which our writer uses of our Lord. He calls Him *Pioneer* of our salvation (2, 10), Pioneer of our faith (12, 2); and in so doing uses a word which occurs elsewhere in the New Testament only in Acts 3, 15 and 5, 31 ("the Pioneer of life" and "this Pioneer and Saviour"). He also refers to Christ as "Forerunner" (6, 20), a word never found elsewhere in the New Testament, but similar to the idea of pioneer. This is our High Priest —One who blazed the trail to God for us to follow. Marcus Dodds, in his commentary on 2, 10, illustrates what is meant by *Pioneer* by comparing him to "the strong swimmer who carries the rope ashore and so not only secures his own position but makes rescue for all who will follow". How splendidly Oscar Cullman gets the thought of the writer when he says of Him who entered the "inner shrine behind the curtain" as "forerunner" that "He draws with Him those who are His into His *Resurrection* and its consequences" (op. cit. p. 101)! That is a phrase worth pondering.

A nineteenth century poetess, Emily Dickinson, shall be the last to suggest to us what Jesus as Pioneer and Forerunner meant to our author and may mean to us:

> "How brittle are the piers
>   On which our faith doth tread,
>   No bridge below doth totter so,
>   Yet none hath such a crowd.
>
> It is as old as God,
>   Indeed, 'twas built by Him;
>   He sent His Son to test the plank,
>   And He pronounced it firm".

(vi) *Shepherd.* Only once does this Epistle refer to Jesus as Shepherd (13, 20). The reference comes in the great closing prayer of the Epistle (vv. 22-25 are a postscript). The writer prays that his readers may be equipped by God to do His will, God working in them to that end. Though they have shown distressing signs of spiritual immaturity and even of apostasy, he does not end on that note. Rather, he turns their eyes away from themselves to God, "the God of peace" and of the resurrection power, and to "our Lord Jesus, the great Shepherd of the sheep". It was through the shedding of His own blood that the new eternal covenant was made and Jeremiah's prophecy (31, 31, quoted in 8, 8 ff. and 10, 16) fulfilled. With His law in their hearts, written in their minds, and their sins and iniquities remembered no more, they will not slip back. They will "lay aside every weight, and sin which clings so closely"

(12, 1). They will "run with patience the race that is set before them", surrounded as they are by a great cloud of witnesses, some of whose names are listed in the noble eleventh chapter, and they will endure as did Jesus, Pioneer and Perfecter, High Priest and great good Shepherd.

This study of the Person of Christ as He is depicted for us in the chapters of this book has given us a key to the understanding of it. It is not the only key, but it is a useful and effective one. It is one which, I believe, is adequate to show that, however uncongenial the language of sacrifice is to a modern reader, the insights of this book are infinitely worth our grappling with, for they expound to us the self-revelation of God to the world in His Son.

V

THE SEER OF THE REVELATION

FOOLS rush in where angels fear to tread. I am fully conscious of this fact as I attempt to do something to open up what to many is a closed book. But I shall make the attempt, for I am convinced that this book, difficult and abstruse as it undoubtedly is at least in part, has got something of very great importance to say, and the sooner we try to find out what that is, the better for us — for us as needy and individual Christians, and for those of us to whom, as preachers, the hungry sheep look up.

Here is this mysterious book. Let us see if, in the goodness of God, some fresh light may break forth from this part of God's word for us, living, as we do, in a day when in the world men's hearts fail them for fear, and in the Church the exercise of our ministry does not, so far as I see, become any easier. Those who are experts in the mysteries of apocalyptic and eschatology must forgive us if we are too elementary for them and if, in the course of this chapter, we by-pass many interesting minutiae of scholarship.

Roughly speaking, we shall divide the book into three main divisions: 1. Chapters 1–5; 2. Chapters 6–19; 3. Chapters 20–22.

It might be as well, at the start, to analyse why we find the understanding and appreciation of such a book as this so difficult. It is, of course, partly our own fault. We read it in disjointed bits, whereas it should be read whole and, as it were, at a run. Ideally it should be read twice or thrice, the reader not worrying too much about details which perplex him, but getting an over-all picture of what the book is about, and allowing the brilliant colours of the book to register on his mind. Let him not stop at the end of chapter three, nor get so discouraged in a welter of seals and trumpets and bowls as to give up the attempt at understanding the book as a bad job. Let him read it in a modern version, not neglecting the very great aid offered to modern readers by Moffatt and Phillips and half a dozen other recent translators. We only make difficulties for ourselves if we will insist on reading this book in a version three and a half centuries old.

But more fundamental as a difficulty which confronts us all is the fact that we are Western and the writer of the *Revelation* was Eastern to his finger-tips. That fact involves us in deep psychological, theological and literary differences. Only when we have made a very real attempt to substitute Oriental for Occidental spectacles shall we be able to read this book (or indeed most of the Biblical books) with any clarity of vision. Let me illustrate what I mean. The Hebrew was no lover of abstracts. He preferred the concrete—a person or a material thing which he could clearly conjure up in his mind's eye. For example, we might say, without fear of being misunderstood: "Beneficence should be unostentatious"—abstract ideas but clear enough to us. A Hebrew, on the other hand, would prefer to put it this way: "When thou doest alms, do not sound a trumpet before thee"; or "Let not thy left hand know what thy right hand doeth"— a series of concrete and vivid and colourful illustrations. Again, we British folk like to pride ourselves on our logicality, our clarity of expression; we have a phrase—"We call a spade a spade". But the Hebrew, for all his love of the concrete, often delights, *not* in saying something direct and outright, but getting his point across by means of parable which stimulates imagination, or by a kind of cipher language. Cipher language does not carry its meaning on the surface; it needs a key to unlock its message. If you have no key, the language makes nonsense.

Another reason why we evade the study of this book is that it has for centuries been the happy hunting-ground for the religious crank; 666 (the number of the Beast—13, 18) can be made to mean anything—the Pope or Martin Luther according to your own religious predilections! The locusts in Chapter 9 which had "tails like unto scorpions, and there were *stings* in their tails" (v. 5, 10) can even, with a measure of ingenuity, be made into bombers carrying a deadly load in their rear! By means of charts and mathematical reckonings, you can even work out a date for the great climax of all things. You can—but if you do so, you will spoil everything and abuse the whole purpose of this book.

It is much more important—and it pays far greater dividends in the understanding of this book—to realise that it is part, perhaps the most profound and superb part, of a great literature that goes under the name of *apocalyptic*. Now do not take alarm at that forbidding word. *You*, though you may not realise it, are apocalyptic in the very way that you are made. At least you were when you were a child. The little girl who was told by her mother that Granny had "gone to live with God", who made no immediate reply, but was heard later to murmur to herself, "Gone to live with God! Gosh! How posh!" was only revealing her apocalyptic nature (though she might not have expressed it that way!). All of us are like prisoners surrounded by a high wall. We ask: "What lies over and beyond?" We long for a ladder—oh for just one peep! The problem of mortality (or is it immortality?), of life and death, of judgement to come, of the final issues of right and wrong! Do St. Augustine and Hitler reach an identical end? Are William Temple and Dr. Goebbels destined for a similar future? Is life:

> "   ...a tale
> Told by an idiot, full of sound and fury,
> Signifying nothing . . ."

Yes, that and no more, if the answers to my questions about Augustine and Hitler, Temple and Goebbels are in the affirmative. But to the extent that we want to know and will not be satisfied without an answer, to that extent we give rein to the *apocalyptic* element which is in the very make-up of every one of us.

I wish that I could speak to you at some length about this very considerable body of literature which we label "apocalyptic". In the Old Testament, the Book of Daniel is the most substantial representative of that literature. But there was a flood of such literature that emanated from Jewish pens during the centuries immediately preceding and following the birth of Christ. We should be mistaken if we view these books as just so many clever productions of ingenious Jewish minds. They were far from that. More often than not, they were literary heart-cries of men who were wrestling with fundamental problems and seeking a way through to an answer. If God was the God whom the prophets had said He was—just, righteous, holy—why did He not vindicate the right? Why was that Hitler of the ancient world, Antiochus Epiphanes, allowed to persecute the Jews as he did, slaughter them, and defile their sanctuary by sacrificing a pig on the holy altar in 168 B.C.? Men, women and children murdered in cold blood—and no intervention from God? Why? Or why was Nero allowed to smear the Christians with tar and set them alight to illumine his gardens as living torches at night? Why did not God send a thunderbolt to stop the profane massacre of Christians as they filed into the arena to satisfy the blood-lust of a mob howling "*Christianos ad leones*"? This is the kind of problem which any thinking man or woman must perforce face to-day if he is to have a philosophy of life or a creed adequate for the task of living and character-building. If we call these books — and not least our own Book of the *Revelation* — "tracts for bad times", we shall not be far wrong. "So far as I can see, the apocalyptic thought that emerged before the opening of the Christian era, and the turn to the kind of speculation which we call eschatological, are . . . a further phase of the search for an interpretation of history which would embrace catastrophe itself and transcend the immediate spectacle of tragedy. Altogether we have here the greatest and most deliberate attempts ever made to wrestle with destiny and interpret history and discover meaning in the human drama; above all, to grapple with the moral difficulties that history presents to the religious mind. The revelation appears not always to have been granted to the ancient Hebrews until there had been a great struggle to achieve the truth" (H. Butterfield, *Christianity and History*, p. 2).

You say: "But why write in such difficult picture language? Why not say clearly what your problem is and what you think is the solution? Why beasts and seals and trumpets and bowls and all the paraphernalia of this extraordinary literature?" The answer is, at least in part, this: A persecuted minority must be very careful about the kind of writing which emanates from it; it must become something of an underground movement if it is to persist at all; it must go to the catacombs, and its very literature must be written in such terms as will be understood by the faithful who have a key, and will not be understood by the persecutors who have no key. Thus, to take but one illustration: I have already referred to "the number of the beast". I think there is little doubt that historically the reference was to *Nero Caesar*, for if the numerical value of the consonants of those two words in their Hebrew form be added up it comes to 666. If a Christian manages to smuggle out of Buchenwald a note to a fellow-Christian at home, the odds are that he will not refer openly to Hitler, but will allude to him by some name or word symbol understood by the persecuted minority. So in the 1st century Rome was alluded to as Babylon (cp. I Peter 5, 13), and Nero as 666.

All this brings us closer to the conditions which gave rise to the book which forms the subject of our study. I am not going to be side-tracked into the byways of discussion—important as they are for a leisurely study of this book—as to the exact date of the *Revelation*. Suffice it for our purpose to say that we can certainly date it in a period of persecution in the 1st century A.D.—such a period as that of Nero's persecution, or of Domitian's near the end of the century. Some would see a combination of literature from both periods. The Christian Church was passing through the fire. The Jews, incensed by what they could not but regard as a blasphemous heresy, sometimes "took it out" on the Christians by "informing" against them to the Romans. The Romans, noticing that the Christians would not collaborate in acts of obedience in the State-religion, suspected this wretched minority of plotting against Caesar. Why should they refuse to worship the Emperor? Why not put a few grains of incense on the fire? Why be so non-collaborationist? Some Christians saw the issues sharply defined—it was Christ or Caesar. Some could not see it that way and, under the pressure of external circumstances and the deceitfulness of their own hearts, found their love growing cold. The second and third generation period was a dangerous one for Christianity, as many of the younger Churches are finding that it is to-day. I think that if we worked in the diocese of Mombasa or Masasi rather than in these islands, we should understand the *Revelation* the more easily.

This, I believe, is the kind of background against which the book of the *Revelation* can alone be understood. It makes the book a much more human document to see it like this. It makes the reader much more patient with its more abstruse passages. Indeed, it enables him to realise that he need not be over-worried if there are passages which we cannot understand for the simple reason that the clue to the cipher-language has been lost—what made sense to the original readers is hidden from us. That may well be true of details. The main lines of the book, however, are, I think, reasonably clear.

I

I have called it a book. It would have been better if I had called it a letter, for a pastoral letter it is, as its beginning and its ending make clear. The letters to the seven churches, which occupy the opening chapters of the book, show an intimate knowledge on the part of the writer of the conditions under which those to whom he writes were living. I suspect that, the better you know the world of the latter decades of the first century, and the more you come to understand the language of our author, the more clearly you will be able to see behind this book a man who knew his Asia Minor and its history and was intimately acquainted with the condition of these young churches which, as the result of missionary work of men like St. Paul, bestrewed the land. Himself an exile on a wretched little island in the Aegean Sea, he set to work probably in a forced labour camp among the mines, his glance often stealing wistfully across the water to the mainland. What would he not have given for the opportunity of joining with one of those congregations on the Lord's Day, of ministering to those whom he knew so well, of checking some faltering Christians and confirming some feeble knees? But it was not to be. What he could do, however, was to set down in apocalyptic language the vision that came to him that "Lord's day", when he "was in the Spirit . . . and heard a great voice behind him, as of a trumpet" (1, 10). So he would warn and encourage his readers. So he would proclaim his Gospel.

It is now for us to see what was the essence of this pastoral message, which, in the form of an apocalyptic vision, John sent to his friends—John who describes himself (1, 9) as "your brother and your companion in the distress, the kingdom and the faithful endurance to which Jesus calls", John who was "on the island called Patmos because I had spoken God's Message and borne witness to Jesus". It is highly significant that the book opens (1, 12–20) with a brilliantly painted picture of Christ in glory. The imagery is majestic and draws heavily on Old Testament language—the Being like a Son of Man, His long robe tied around His breast to indicate work completed, His eyes blazing, His feet shining, His voice like the sound of a great waterfall, and a sharp two-edged sword coming out of His mouth. He declares Himself to be the First and the Last, the One who was dead but is alive for ever, holding in His own powerful hand those little, trembling, persecuted churches of Asia Minor. They need not fear—they were in His hand!

It shows the keen spiritual insight and the sure touch of the Seer that he begins his message where he does—with a vision of the Living Christ. *That* was the answer, the only effective answer, to those who were sore tempted and were lapsing from their faith. Let them see Him in the nearness and the awefulness of His Majesty—"fear not. *I am* . . ." When in 1955, I mixed with African Christians who had been tempted in ways very similar to those which tempted their first century brethren, I found that those who withstood the Mau Mau atrocities were those who kept clear before them the vision of the Risen Christ with the seven stars in His right hand. It is ever so. Apostasy occurs—in Mission field and in home parish—when the figure of our Lord is allowed to become dim in the eyes of the people. To put it concretely—if the Seventh Day Adventists and the Christian Scientists and other strange "deviations" flourish in any given area, it is time for us to look to our laurels and to ask the question: Is the Person of Jesus, in all His glory and fulness, being uplifted in this district? Let Christology become flabby and Christolatry become weak, and it will not be long before the lamp of Christian discipleship burns dim.

I must not delay long over chapters 2 and 3, for they are probably the chapters in this book with which you are most familiar. I will content myself with a few comments which may serve to send some of you back to a fresh study of those letters to the seven churches of Asia. They are seven gems, which shine the more brightly the better you know the history and geography of the places to which they were addressed. Old as Sir William Ramsay's *Letters to the Seven Churches* now is (it was published by Hodder & Stoughton in 1904), I commend it to you if you want to understand the background of these letters. If you are looking for something shorter, and if you have access to Hastings' *Dictionary of the Bible*, Ramsay's articles on the individual places to which the letters are addressed are well worth consulting.

First, it is clear that the writer knows very intimately the circumstances of the churches to which he writes—their stresses and strains, their temptations, their failures and their triumphs. There is a firm and tender pastoral touch about each of the letters.

Secondly, there is a pattern common to all the letters.

Each is addressed to the "angel" (does this mean leader? Or delegate? Or the composite personality of the Church as seen by God?). Then is given a characteristic of the Speaker— "these things saith He who . . ." Then come the words "I know . . .". The message ends with the words "He that hath an ear . . ." and with a promise to him who is victorious. This is the framework in which each gem is set.

Thirdly, I would comment briefly on what we have just noticed—that at the beginning of each letter comes a characteristic of the divine Speaker. This characteristic is drawn from the vision of the Risen Christ which was given in Chapter 1. Thus, the attention of the Ephesians (2, 1) is drawn to Him "that holdeth the seven stars in His right hand" (1, 16); the attention of the Smyrnaeans (2, 8) to "the First and the Last, which was dead and is alive" (1, 17 and 18); the attention of the church in Pergamum (2, 12) to Him "which hath the sharp sword with two edges" (1, 16), and so on. To each Church, the living Lord *is* what it needs (whether of comfort or of judgement or of both), *speaks* what it needs, and *promises* what it needs.

Lastly, I bid you ponder the fact I have just mentioned— that the content of every letter begins with the words "*I know* . . ." Those whose task it is to read these letters in public will recall that a good deal of care is called for in the reading of them. The words "I know . . ." can convey a variety of meaning, depending on the tone in which they are read. Sometimes the words carry the tone of sympathetic understanding, sometimes of stern cognisance of sin and failure, always of the knowledge and insight of Him whose "eyes were as a flame of fire" (1, 14).

Chapters 4 and 5 are something of a unity. The Seer sees a door opened in heaven (you must be prepared for anything in apocalyptic literature—nothing must surprise you!); and a trumpet-like voice bids him come up and be

shown "what must happen in the future". So, like a
military commander mounting a hill the better to get an
over-all picture of the battle, the Seer mounts — and looks —
and listens. He tells us what he sees — a vision of God and of
the Lamb. He tells us what he hears — first the *trisagion*
("Holy, holy, holy, Lord God Almighty" — 4, 8); secondly
the new song ("Thou art worthy . . . for Thou wast slain
and hast redeemed us to God by Thy blood" — 5, 9 ff.);
and, thirdly, the universal song ("Blessing and honour and
glory and power be unto Him that sitteth upon the throne,
and unto the Lamb for ever and ever"). Incidentally, we
have here an interesting illustration of the fact that these
early Christians, long before a careful Trinitarian theology
was worked out and long before the early heresies had
forced them to hammer out a precise theology, knew that:

> "The highest place which heaven affords
> Is His, is His by right;
> The King of kings and Lord of lords
> And heaven's eternal light".

This, then, is the general setting of Chapters 4 and 5, in
sight and in sound. But at the heart of the passage is a
problem — and its solution. To that we must now turn our
attention.

The problem is set before us in the form of a scroll, with
writing inside and out, but sealed with seven seals (5, 1).
The Seer was in tears because no one could be found who
was able to open the scroll or look inside it. The problem
was, as we should say, insoluble by human skill or ingenuity — indeed "there was no one in heaven or on earth or
under the earth able to open the scroll". It was at that
moment of human extremity that one of the elders said
to the Seer: "Do not weep, for the Lion from the tribe of
Judah, the Root of David, has won the right to open the

scroll and break its seven seals". We wait, in the apocalyptic drama, to see the Lion appear, the king of beasts, the symbol of limitless power. But we wait in vain. Instead there appears on the scene—a Lamb with the marks of slaughter upon it! (5, 6). True, it has seven horns (which speak of power). True, it has seven eyes (which speak of knowledge). But a Lamb it is—the symbol of meekness and gentleness, the symbol of sacrifice and suffering unto death. "He is brought as a lamb to the slaughter, and as a sheep before her shearers is dumb, so he openeth not his mouth". So we read in Isaiah 53. This is the Seer's identification of the prophet's mysterious figure. Here is power indeed, but power interpreted in terms of gentleness and sacrifice; and this it is which *prevails*.

You ask what *is* this scroll sealed with seven seals? The writer of the Revelation does not answer in so many words. In this he was like his Master who, to the annoyance of His questioners, often refused to give a straight answer to a straight question, in order to make them think again. "What do *you* think?" He would counter. We humans are lazy creatures, and God is good to make us think again, treating us as adults rather than as children who have to be told that two and two equal four.

What *is* this scroll sealed with seven seals? Perhaps there is no one clear, water-tight answer. Perhaps the answer can best be approximated if we remember that Jesus taught in parables, and that there is an "elasticity" about parables which allows of several interpretations to any one parable. Who, for example, is to say that when Jesus spoke of the pearl of great price He meant precisely *this* and not *that*? May it not be that He meant *both*—and a great deal more; and left *us* to think it all out?

This scroll sealed with seven seals—is it the Old Testament, mysterious, enigmatic, awful with the terrors of Sinai, until the Lamb does for us what Jesus did for the disciples on the road to Emmaus—opens the Scriptures and expounds in all the Scriptures the things concerning Himself (St. Luke 24, 27)? Is it the hidden Name of God, the ineffable Name that might not be spoken—"I am that I am", or, more probably, "I will become what I will become" (Exodus 3, 14)? "Verily Thou art a God that hidest Thyself" (Isaiah 45, 15). There is a moving passage in Gerhard von Rad's *Moses* in which he deals with the problem of the ineffable Name of God. "The Name of God in the Old Testament brings us face to face with a strange and perplexing mystery. Men know that Name and utter it; and yet, in relation to it, they are like men standing on the edge of a precipice. Here is a Name. Implied in this Name is a revelation of God filled to the brim with grace and with God's freedom to forgive; and yet at the same time this revelation entices man, in the secret depths of his being, to try to lay violent hands upon it; it seems to stimulate that rebellious element that is present in every man. Is it surprising that in the end the problem was solved by taking this Name out of the mouths of men, and absolutely forbidding them ever to utter it? But this was not in reality a solution. It only meant that the mystery was sealed up. Then came the time when the books of the Old Testament were collected, and were bound together by the iron clasp of the Canon; and so the inheritance and the harvest of the whole story of God's salvation, as it had been wrought in the days of the Old Testament, was shut away and sealed up in a book. And at its heart, like the soul and the secret of the meaning of the book, lay the mystery of the most holy Name of God. Who will break the seal, and reveal the mystery?" Von Rad's closing words bring us back to the book of *Revelation*. The Seer would say what the writer of the Gospel says in even more plain language—"No man hath seen God at any time; the only begotten Son . . . He hath *declared* Him" (St. John 1, 18), given us the true exegesis of Him. "The Lamb hath prevailed to open the book."

The problem of the Old Testament and of the hidden Name of God—that, it may well be, is contained in the problem of the scroll sealed with seven seals. But I think there is more to it than that. The position of this chapter in the over-all plan of the book would clearly suggest that this sealed scroll represents the *why* of a suffering world and of a persecuted Church. This chapter is immediately succeeded by the vision of the four horse-men which, as we shall see, represent conquering ambition, war, famine, and death. These are the very things which have blasted mankind since Cain slew his brother Abel, and which threaten us in unprecedented fury to-day. Man's inhumanity to man; lust, oppression, crime. From one angle, how sordid a thing is the tale of human history! Thank God, the Seer would say to us that the scroll is in the Hands of Him Who sits on the throne; that is to say, God has not abdicated from history. Its problems are not ignored in the courts of heaven. There is a promise of solution there. But there is no answer until the Lion-Lamb prevails to open the scroll and break its seven seals.

I cannot leave this vision of the sealed scroll without a further word. Man to-day lives in a universe far more vast than the universe that the Seer ever dreamed of—far more vast and far more terrifying. If Blaise Pascal in the seventeenth century could speak of the terrifying nature of the *silence* of the infinite spaces, how much more does twentieth century man appreciate the reference! And he is the discoverer of the means of harnessing the physical power at the heart of the universe. Sometimes he feels like a small baby wielding naked razor blades! "We are", says F. R. Barry in his remarkable book *Asking the Right Questions*, "we are terribly, even dangerously clever and can offer glib judgements about almost everything; but the unconscious hungers are being starved and are therefore seeking illusory satisfactions, whether in violence or in sexuality. This schism in the mind of man is the radical malaise of the West. Most of our frustrations and neuroses originate in this hunger for meaning which our intellect seems to condemn to remain unsatisfied. Imperatively we must learn how to follow the hints of that still largely invisible document. But have we the code — the key by which to decipher it and so understand the meaning of the whole?" (p. 138). Note the bishop's phrase — "this hunger for meaning". Later in his book he elaborates the thesis that it is the claim of the Christian revelation to satisfy precisely this hunger. The eternal Logos of the Fourth Gospel *is* "the divine purpose or 'meaning' of creation, that makes sense of the total cosmic process" (p. 161-2). Barry goes on to say: "That does not mean, of course, that Christianity professes to answer any or every conundrum in heaven or earth . . . Nor does it mean that the Church has privileged access to facts about the physical universe and can go behind the backs of the scientists. That is not what Christianity offers. What it offers is light enough to live by and the true light in which men can see. And the claim is that, looking out on the world of human experience in the light of Christ, Christian thought can interpret and make sense of it because it discerns through that revelation the ultimate purpose and meaning of the whole drama" (p. 162). Is it not this claim which the Seer is making in this vision of the sealed book, which only the Lion-Lamb prevailed to open?

Look once again at the imagery of the Lion of the tribe of Judah who is also the Lamb with the marks of slaughter upon it. Here is strange paradox indeed! (We meet such paradox again later in the book in the phrase "the wrath of the Lamb" (6, 16) — a paradox if ever there was one!). We shall be noticing later the principle of antithesis which runs through the book of the *Revelation*. Here we have it at its clearest. The forces of evil in this book are described under the imagery of a Beast. It is of the nature of a wild beast, red in tooth and claw, to seize, to snatch, to kill, to grasp for itself and for itself alone. It is of the nature of the Lamb to empty itself of life in sacrificial giving. "The divine nature was His from the first; yet He did not think to snatch at equality with God, but made Himself nothing, assuming the nature of a slave ... He humbled Himself, and in obedience accepted even death—death on a cross". (Philippians 2, 6–8). "He was oppressed, and he was afflicted, yet he opened not his mouth; he is brought as a lamb to the slaughter, and as a sheep before her shearers is dumb so he openeth not his mouth" (Isaiah 53, 7).

What does all this amount to? It amounts to this—that we find light on the problem of the Old Testament, and of the ineffable Name, on the *why* of a suffering world and of a persecuted Church, on the meaning of creation that makes sense of the total cosmic process, not so much in the teaching of a Galilean prophet as in the Cross where the Lamb of God died, the Lamb with the marks of slaughter upon it.

Mrs. Hamilton King, in a too little known poem *The Disciples*, takes up this theme, particularly in a long section entitled *Ugo Bassi*. She uses, not indeed the figure of the slain Lamb but of the bleeding Vine as her illustration, but the truth in both pictures is essentially the same. Fra Ugo Bassi was a member of the Order of St. Barnabas living in the nineteenth century in Rome and exercising his ministry in the great hospital, taking:

> "His turn in preaching, at the service held
>   Where five long chambers, lined with suffering folk,
> Converged..."

He takes his text from St. John, "I am the Vine; ye are the branches":

> "The Living Vine, Christ chose it for Himself:
> God gave to man for use and sustenance
> Corn, wine, and oil, and each of these is good
> And Christ is Bread of Life, and Light of Life;
> But yet He did not choose the summer corn,
> That shoots up straight and free in one quick growth,
> And has its day, and is done, and springs no more:
> Nor yet the olive, all whose boughs are spread
> In the soft air, and never lose a leaf,
> Flowering and fruitful in perpetual peace:
> But only this for Him and His in one —
> The everlasting, ever quickening Vine,
> That gives the heat and passion of the world,
> Through its own life-blood, still renewed and shed".

And so he draws his lesson:

> "Measure thy life by loss instead of gain;
> Not by the wine drunk, but the wine poured forth;
> For love's strength standeth in love's sacrifice;
> And whoso suffers most hath most to give".

That is the lesson, as I see it, which comes to us from the Christ in glory whom we see in Chapter 1; from the Christ of Chapters 2 and 3 whose knowledge of the Churches is as intimate as His love for them is never-dying; from the Christ of Chapters 4 and 5 who, sharing the throne with the Father, prevails, as the Lion-Lamb, to open the book sealed hitherto to all but Himself, but now open for those who are one with Him and in whom is the mind which was also in Christ Jesus "who humbled Himself and became obedient unto death".

The great central section of the book of the *Revelation*, chapters 6-19 which constitute the second of its three main divisions, is the toughest and most difficult part of the Apocalypse. It will, I think, become easier to us if we continue to remember that it is possible that at certain points the key to unlock the cipher language may have got lost. We must not, therefore, be over troubled if there are certain minor passages which do not yield their meaning to us, or on which commentators differ greatly. It will also become easier to us if we give careful attention to the main *plan* of this central section, and to certain *principles* (such as those of climax, of parenthesis and of antithesis) by which the Seer's work is governed.

First, then, the *plan*. A large part of this central section is given up to depicting three great series of visions of judgement; and to those we shall come shortly. The last of these series comes in Chapter 16. Then follows the vision of the fall of the Beast (Chapters 17 and 18) and, immediately after, what we might call the Hallelujah chorus (19). (Here let me say, in passing, that this book has been a great theme for the musicians and, incidentally, for the artists. If you find yourself wanting to sing, as you study this book, that is not to be wondered at. The book itself is bestrewn with songs which rise from the courts of heaven (4, 8 and 11; 5, 9-10, 12; 7, 12; 11, 15 and 17-18), from every created thing in heaven and on earth and in the sea (5, 13), and from the vast throng of the redeemed which no man could number (7, 9). Grim as the conflict undoubtedly is, persecuted and harried as the Church is, the final triumph is assured and is celebrated in song, song which reaches its climax in the Hallelujah chorus of Chapter 19 (vv. 1-2, 3, 4, 5, 7-8).

We may now come to the three series of visions of judgement, the vision of the seals, the trumpets and the bowls ("vials" in A.V.). The references are important and should be noted carefully:

The vision of the seven seals occupies Chapters 6 and 8, 1.

The vision of the seven trumpets occupies Chapters 8, 2–end, 9 and 11, 15–19.

The vision of the seven bowls of the wrath of God occupies Chapter 16.

As we read these three series of judgements we note that they depict a mounting cataclysm—each series is worse, more terrifying, than that which precedes it. Anderson Scott calls the approach of the writer "spiral"—the further he advances with it and the higher he mounts, the more he can see and the more fearful the judgements appear to be. Indeed, the colours of his pictures would be well-nigh unbearable if it were not for the principle of parenthesis which he introduces and which we shall examine shortly.

But first let us look at the vision of the seven seals, and then I shall very largely leave it to you to examine the other two series, which follow it.

The subject was introduced to us—but only touched on —in Chapter 5, 1, the scroll with writing inside and out, but sealed with seven seals. In Chapter 6 we watch the opening of six of these seven seals, but we have to wait till 8, 1 for the opening of the seventh. The first four are the four horsemen. The first (6, 1–2) rides a *white* horse and represents invasion, or, more generally, selfish ambition, "the lust of gain is the spirit of Cain". The second (6, 3–4) rides a *red* horse and represents war, the bloody follower of invasion. The third (6, 5–6) rides a *black* horse and represents famine. Food is scarce, the amount of flour that one man would eat in a day costs a full day's wage, while comparative luxuries like olives and wine are cheap. The fourth rides a *sickly pale* horse and represents death, the inevitable follower of invasion, war, and famine; death, with Hades in close attendance.

Such, then, is the vision disclosed by the breaking of the first four seals, the weary story of man's inhumanity to man, of which our own generation has sampled the fury more terribly than any of its predecessors. The war of 1939 –45 was—potentially, at least—much worse than that of 1914-18. It would, however, be but a flea-bite compared with any major conflict that might succeed it; but did we not note that the Seer's approach to history and judgement was *spiral*?

The breaking of the fifth seal (6, 9–11) discloses to us the sight, underneath (or, at the foot of) the altar, of the souls of those who had been slaughtered for God's word and for their testimony to Him. They join in the age-long cry— "How long?" And they are told that they must wait a little longer until the tally of Christ's martyrs should be complete.

The breaking of the sixth seal (6, 12–end) shows us an earthquake—a vast upheaval in sky and sea and on earth. The language is typical apocalyptic language, and reminds us of such passages in the Gospels as St. Matthew 24, 29, 30, St. Mark 13, etc.

The breaking of the seventh seal is delayed until 8, 1. We expect, if it were possible, something more terrible than what the first six visions have disclosed. Surprisingly, we get nothing of the kind. We get *silence* in heaven, a silence, however, not of peace, but a stillness such as that which precedes a great thunderstorm, a silence big with fate. And before we have time to settle down or be lulled by the silence into a false sense of security, we are launched into the next series of judgements, that of the trumpets, which proves to be even more severe than that of the seals.

Of the visions of the trumpets and of the bowls I would say only a little. In a sense, each series is complete in itself,

78

and seems to bring us to the verge of the end of all. Then from the end of the first springs a second series, and from the end of the second a third. If one may illustrate the awful of *Revelation* by the beautiful of Beethoven, the latter's Fifth Symphony seems about to end many times, but then bursts out again. So it is with the *Revelation*. It is the principle of climax—all the series of judgements bring "exhibitions of the same principle under different aspects and in different circumstances" (W. Milligan, *Lectures on the Apocalypse*, p. 104). "As sin deepens, judgement deepens" (op. cit., p. 109). Perhaps it is the Seer's method of preparing the Church for a long-drawn-out period of suffering, while at the same time he conveys the idea of mounting horror. On a vast scale, and by the use of startling and vivid colours, the writer works out the familiar idea of the "pangs of the Messiah", that is to say, the idea that the Messiah's coming would be preceded by a succession of disasters in which the present order will be swept away.

A quick glance at the vision of the trumpets shows us nature (the first four, 8, 2 ff.) and the powers of hell (the fifth and sixth trumpets, Chapter 9) as media of punishment. We note similarities to the story of the plagues of Egypt in Exodus, and we remember that John's vision came to him, lonely as he was, on the horrid storm-tossed island of Patmos. In regard to the demonic judgements of Chapter 9, we may remark that in Jewish thought the forces of evil are never totally outside of God's control. If this "is hell let *loose*, it is hell *let* loose" (H. L. Goudge, *The Apocalypse and the Present Age*, p. 82). The last trumpet vision, for which we have to wait until Chapter 11, 15-19, shows us the Reign of God and the submission of the kingdoms of this world. We feel that we have reached the end—but the end is not yet!

We may now pass from the three visions of series of

judgements with their elaboration of the principle or climax, to notice two further principles by which the writer is guided in his work. He uses the principle of *parenthesis* with great effect. Just as a musician may introduce a little light movement between two weightier ones, and (if the parallel be allowed) as a dramatist introduces a fool to caper on the stage between two scenes of great and lengthy tension, so the Seer, when our nerves are stretched to breaking-point and his visions of judgement prove well-nigh unbearable, introduces a parenthesis for our relief. Let me illustrate. Chapter 7 is one such parenthesis. We have watched the breaking of six seals and are expecting the seventh, when we find that we have to wait. The interval is occupied with the gracious vision of the 144,000 of those who carried the seal of God in their foreheads, and of the vast throng from every nation and kindred and people and tongue who "have come through the great oppression and washed their robes and made them white in the blood of the Lamb" and who, for that reason and that alone, "stand before the Throne of God, and serve Him day and night in His Temple". Then follows that astonishingly moving passage: "They shall hunger no more, neither thirst any more; neither shall the sun light on them, nor any heat. For the Lamb which is in the midst of the throne shall feed them, and shall lead them unto living fountains of waters: and God shall wipe away all tears from their eyes" (7, 16, 17).

Or again, the principle of parenthesis may be illustrated by the way in which the writer, having given us six of the seven trumpet visions in chapters 8 and 9, keeps us waiting for the seventh until the end of Chapter 11. Thus he relieves tension and at the same time keeps us expectant. Somewhat similarly, Chapter 15, verse 1 introduces us to the seven last plagues, but we have to wait till Chapter 16 to know precisely what these are. The story is interrupted by the parenthetical vision of those who had won the victory over the beast and its image and were singing the song of Moses and of the Lamb—"great and marvellous are thy works, Lord God Almighty; just and true are thy ways, thou King of saints. Who shall not fear thee, O Lord, and glorify thy name? For thou only art holy: for all nations shall come and worship before thee; for thy judgements are made manifest" (15, 3, 4).

I pass now to another principle which we see at work in the *Revelation*—the principle of *antithesis*. I shall say something later about the Seer's philosophy of history. Suffice it now to say that he is deeply conscious of the fact that a fearful fight is being waged and will continue to be waged until history as we know it is wound up. It is this deep conviction which lies at the back of the series of contrasts which run throughout his book. Again I illustrate:

Fundamentally, the conflict may be described as a battle joined between God and Satan. There is the basic antithesis of the book. Perhaps that might be elaborated as a battle between the Blessed Trinity and the Devil, the Beast and the false prophet (Chs. 12 and 13). (If it be objected that a reference to the Trinity is hardly justifiable, we may at least note the reference in 1, 4, 5, to "Him Who is . . ., the seven spirits . . ., and Jesus Christ"). As the Father commissions the Son (1, 1), so the Dragon gives the Beast power, rule and authority (13, 2).

The Lamb is seen in antithesis to the Beast; the emblem of weakness, of suffering and of sacrifice over against that creature whose nature it is to snatch, to seize, to despoil.

The numberless company of the redeemed is offset by the hosts of wickedness; the believers sealed with the seal of their God upon their foreheads (7, 3) by those who bear the beast's mark (13, 16).

The bride, the Lamb's wife (21), in all her purity, stands out in brilliant contrast to the harlot, the great whore in all her filthy shame (17). "The holy city, new Jerusalem, coming down from God out of heaven" (21, 2) offsets Babylon (17 and 18), "mother of harlots and abominations of the earth" (17, 5).

The name of the Son is Jesus, Joshua the great deliverer. The name of the agent of evil is in Hebrew Abaddon, in Greek Apollyon — "destruction" (9, 11).

You can continue the list as you study the book. Antithesis, together with climax and parenthesis, is not the least effective of the principles, the stylistic devices, of which the Seer makes use.

Before I come to say something about the closing chapters of this second section and the description here given of Babylon, I feel I must say something to you about a perplexing feature of the book we are studying. I refer to the Seer's use of *numbers*. There is, I think, a real danger lest we bring in here mathematical precision where the Seer intends only symbolic significance; lest we *calculate* where he would only *indicate*. Our Western logic must not lead us to forget or to ignore Eastern filmy mysticism. I believe that we do far better to seek for certain principles which underlie the Seer's use of numbers generally, than to take out our logarithm tables and work out dates! Thus when St. John writes of the number of the beast (13, 18) and says that the number represents a man's name, I have little doubt that he is referring to Nero Caesar, for when we add up the immediate value of the letters which comprise these two words they do total 666. But I am pretty sure that the writer sees a deeper and more subtle significance. Seven is the perfect number, but 666 is at every point *short* of perfection. Again, when the Seer writes of the 144,000 of those who had received the seal of God in their foreheads (7, 4), we should look for the significance of the figure 12 in the mind of a Hebrew-Christian, for 144,000 is 12 x 12 taken a thousandfold. We need not look for long. There were 12 tribes, 12 Apostles who would sit on 12 thrones. The city has 12 gates, and so on. This is the number of God's People, and its multiplication by 12 and by 1000 underlines the fact that it is a vast number who will have this sign in their forehead. Perhaps, also, in the 24 elders who surrounded the throne of God (4, 4) we may see a hint of the 12 Apostles and the twelve patriarchs united, New Testament church and Old Testament church now one in worship.

Or again, if 7 is the number of perfection and completion, three and a half has probably a sinister significance — it is seven *broken*. Thus the 42 months (13, 5) during which it was given to the Beast to make war upon the followers of the Lamb, the "time and times and half a time" of 12, 14, and the 1260 days of 11, 3 — all these references come in passages whose context is gloomy and bloody. The number 10 seems also to hold a sinister significance to the mind of the Seer — the Christians of Smyrna suffer persecution for 10 days (2, 10); the dragon, the Beast of the Sea, the Scarlet Beast have 10 hours, and so on. As to the figure 1000, as Erskine Hill says (*Mystical Studies in the Apocalypse*, p. 192), it "presents a hazardous problem, millenial and perennial, and one which has been responsible for much writing which is both fanciful and absurd". I am inclined to associate myself with his next sentence: "Of one thing we may be quite sure, that the figure, while referring to a long-extended period of time, is not meant to be definite". If that be so, it is but in keeping with all that I have just been saying.

Let me add a word on the way in which our writer speaks of the evil which he sees is threatening the Church. Behind all this cipher language of Beast, of serpent, of Babylon, and so on, what are the dread realities that he is thinking about? For myself I have no doubt that they were ultimately connected with the precise historical situation in which St. John found himself. "The (Roman) Empire is the revelation of the dragon, as the Lord is the revelation of the Father" (H. L. Goudge, op. cit., p. 93). It was the incarnation of might, ruling by force, whereas the Kingdom of God rules by love. There is, in this apocalyptic writing, a constant merging of the two ideas of the Empire and the man who finally represents it, and these are inseparable from the idea of Satan himself. (We can still use the words Nazism and Hitler more or less interchangeably.) There are references, I think, also to an imperial priesthood, invested with full powers to enforce Emperor worship (see especially 13, 11–18, a passage to which Kiddle (*Moffatt Commentary*, p. 256) gives the suggestive title: "Universal Inquisition, performed by the Priests of Antichrist").

Is there anything in literature quite like Chapters 17 and 18 for a description of the forces of tyranny concentrated in Rome? I doubt it. Tacitus described Rome as the city where "all kinds of enormity and filthy shame meet together and become fashionable". He was not far wrong. Rome is described as a woman (cities are generally *feminine*), a harlot, a gorgeous mother of evil, dressed in imperial purple and scarlet, glittering with gold, jewels and pearls (17, 4). She is seated upon many waters (17, 1), symbol of Rome's domination over many nations. The name written on her forehead is Babylon the Great— Babylon, which Sir George Adam Smith described as "the Atheist of the Old Testament, the Anti-Christ of the New" (*Isaiah*, Volume ii, p. 188 ff.). She is drunk, but not with wine; she is drunk with the blood of the saints and of the martyrs for Jesus (17, 6). She rides upon a scarlet animal, whose seven heads are the seven hills on which Rome is planted. These seven hills represent the seven Emperors on whose authority the city's power is broadly based. "Five of them are fallen"—Augustus, Tiberius,

Caligula, Claudius and Nero; "one is" namely Vespasian; "the other is not yet come", that is, Titus is not yet on the throne. So runs one quite possible interpretation. The reference to the Beast that "was, and is not, and is about to come up out of the abyss" (17, 8) is very probably to Nero of whom there were terrifying rumours that, *redivivus*, he would return—horrid thought! "The Woman that you saw is the Great City which dominates the kings of the earth" (17, 18). That is Chapter 17. Chapter 18 describes her fall. With the faith of true prophetic insight, the Seer sees her ruined—trade gone (18, 11 ff.); social life gone (18, 22); light gone (18, 23); shattered to nought, like a millstone hurled into the sea of God's wrath (18, 21). And a great cry goes up from the Church of God: "Alleluia!" (19, 1 ff.). "The Lord God omnipotent reigneth" (19, 6).

As to the fulfilment of this prophecy of Rome's destruction, I would say this: faith is, in a sense, like the God whom it worships, supra-temporal. Rome's destruction did not come in a night. It came gradually, partly through decay, and then, at the end, suddenly by the invasion of the Goths early in the 5th Century (A.D. 410 to be exact). It came also through the gradual triumph of the Church, that insignificant little handful of harried, tortured believers, that trembling "little flock" of Christ whose faith was like some tiny seed which, growing into a tree, broke up the foundations of a mighty building.

3

The book of the *Revelation*, in addition to being a pastoral letter (as we saw at the start of this chapter) claims to be a *prophecy* ("this book of prophesy", 22, 19). It is of the nature of prophecy that its primary reference should be to some particular historical situation. Thus, the prophecies of Amos are coloured through and through by the historical events which were going on around him in the eighth century B.C., in his own country and in the neighbouring countries, Ammon, Moab and so on. Against that particular background he uttered the word of the Lord. But it is equally of the nature of Biblical prophecy not to have its message exhausted by that particular historical reference. On the contrary, prophecy is concerned with truths which are of eternal and universal relevance. That is why the Old Testament prophetical books are very much alive to-day for those who have ears to hear and eyes to see.

It is so with the book of the *Revelation*. As we saw earlier, it had its origin in a particular historical situation of great and poignant difficulty to the Church. St. John, when he spoke of Babylon and the Beast, of the harlot and the horned animals, saw the enemy as clearly as did Dietrich Bonhoeffer when he wrote *The Cost of Discipleship* against the awful background of the Nazi régime which eventually led him to his death on April 9th, 1945. But—and this is the main point of the closing parts of this chapter—when we have reconstructed the historical situation, when we have placed the *Revelation* firmly in the second half of the first century, when we have identified Beast and false prophet and all the rest of it, we have only begun our work. For this, let me repeat, is *prophecy*, and prophecy has a word for all time, dealing as it does, not only with the local and the particular, but with universal truth. What, then, I would ask, has the *Revelation* to say to us in the twentieth century, called to bear our witness (and to preach our message) in conditions so very different from the catacomb conditions of the first decades of the Church's life? It would take a book to answer that question. I can but indicate the directions in which an answer is to be found, and leave you to work out the implications.

I believe that this book has a word to say to us about the

nature of history, and it is of great importance that we should hear the word, believe it, and act accordingly. Its view of history is a realistic, even a sombre view. It faces the sinister element in human nature with an almost terrifying frankness, faces it unblinking and unafraid. The Seer comes to grips with the evil which he finds in the world. He advances no facile theory of a society which, given a little effort and some further education, will pull itself up by its bootstrings. He does not see Utopia round the corner. True, he sees, with the eye of faith, the ultimate triumph of God and of His Christ. But that is not yet. Meanwhile, the fight becomes increasingly stern, and the colours of war and of judgement increasingly dark.

It is strange how slow modern man—both inside the Church and outside it—is in coming to terms with this insight of the Seer's, and how easily he becomes the slave of wishful thinking about the nature of man, of society, and of history. I venture to think that St. John's approach to history should be more easily understood by us who live in the awful aftermath of two world wars and under the Damocletian sword of the threat of a third, than it was by our fathers who lived in the first secure decade of this century. But I am not at all sure how seriously the diabolical element is taken by the average man. When a clergyman some time ago came to see me, and showed himself shocked and disillusioned by the callousness and carelessness of those among whom he had worked, he told me that his father had brought him up to believe that all men were good. I said: "What a pity he didn't teach you the New Testament." Do you recall the second chapter of Professor Herbert Butterfield's *Christianity and History*? It is entitled "Human Nature in History". Its last two sentences read: "It is essential not to have faith in human nature. Such faith is a recent heresy and a very disastrous one." But the whole chapter deserves careful study. I

87

must not quote at length, but almost at random let me quote a few sentences: "Lord Acton said that practically all great men were bad men and that hardly any public reputation survived the exposure of private archives. I think he would have been kinder if he had made the whole world kin, and would have been less unbalanced himself if he had started simply on the footing that all men are sinners" (p. 29). "Down below there slumbers all the time the volcano that lies in human nature, and an unexpected cataclysm may bring it into activity" (p. 31). "If there is an aspect of the modern tragedy which is to be regretted, because it might conceivably have been avoided, it is that the last generation suffered so much from the superficiality of its idealists and the spiritual impoverishment of its self-styled prophets. It seems to me that some of the most inveterate talkers during my lifetime have been the victims of precisely that optical illusion on the subject of human nature which I have described; and we have gambled very highly on what was an over-optimistic view of the character of man" (pp. 33–34).

What, then, of the final triumph so movingly depicted in the closing chapters of the *Revelation*? Is this just a happy ending — "they all lived happily ever after"? Or is it something infinitely more profound than this? No one could maintain that Bishop Charles Gore was a facile optimist. Indeed, he might have been charged with having within him a certain streak of pessimism. But he maintained that deep down in the heart of Christianity there was ground for what he called an "ultimate optimism". That last phrase would sum up the philosophy of history given to us in the *Revelation*, a philosophy based on a fundamental theology of Resurrection. (Perhaps one of the most interesting passages where Gore works at this theme is in his *Belief in Christ*, pp. 156–60 (1924 edition).)

Towards the end of his strange book, *The Invading*

Gospel, Jack Clemo writes (pp. 138 ff.): "The whole philosophy of Christian optimism is founded on the literal resurrection of Christ, the fact that His triumph was a part of His earthly and corporeal existence. When those feet last walked our earth they were not the feet of a sufferer, a Man of Sorrow. When that voice last spoke it did not say, 'My God, why hast Thou forsaken me?' . . . The feet moved briskly across the shore to a picnic in the spring dawn; the voice asked playfully, 'Children, have ye any meat?' . . . Truth did not for ever stay on the scaffold: Truth came down from the scaffold, walked out of the tomb and ate boiled fish."

This view of history, realistic, even sombre, but finally optimistic, is based on a vigorous and powerful doctrine of God and of Christ. It would be true to say that the tenderer aspects of the character of God are soft-pedalled in this book. That is not to say that they are entirely absent. Far from it. What tenderer saying in all Scripture is there than this — "God shall wipe away all tears from their eyes" (7, 17)? Nevertheless, it is the transcendence and majesty of God which stand out pre-eminently. He is an awe-inspiring figure — the "One who is and who was and who is to come" (1, 4, 8; 4, 8; *not* 11, 17 in the best texts). He is the "sovereign Lord of all" (1, 8 etc. The word which is used nine times in the *Revelation* occurs only once elsewhere in the New Testament, II Corinthians, 6, 18, itself a quotation from the Old). He is the faithful, the mighty, the First and the Last. So adjective is piled on adjective to convey the over-all impression of supreme, transcendent majesty.

But He is also a God who is intensely active in history. When St. John describes Him as the one "who is to come", he does not use a mere future participle of the verb to be. He calls Him "the Coming One". This is the God of whom the Psalmist wrote when he said: "Our God *comes*, he does not keep silence" (Psalm 50, 3 R.S.V.). He is not aloof from the flux of human history, with all its agonies and frustrations. He is made known to man in the Person of Him who, in a particular historical situation at Bethlehem and Calvary, *came down* for us men and for our salvation. If the thrice repeated "I am coming soon" of the last chapter (22, 7, 12, 20) has a strictly eschatological reference, it is spoken by One who in history has always been coming and is coming yet, coming in saving power and in judgement.

This God, omniscient, omnipotent, all-sovereign, all-active, is the centre of ceaseless worship—worship which would continue if this world ceased to spin. "The Bible is the book in which the glory of God is the first concern, and the salvation of man comes second" (E. Brunner: *The Mediator*, p. 408). If this is true of the Bible as a whole, it is certainly true of its last book.

Richard Niebuhr once parodied the kind of God preached in certain American pulpits. "A God without wrath brought men without sin into a kingdom without judgment through the ministrations of a Christ without a Cross" (*The Kingdom of God in America*, p. 193). This is certainly not the God of the *Revelation*. Here is no senti-mental grandfather. Here is power and majesty, at work in judging and saving activity.

What of the Person of our Lord as He is depicted for us in this book? St. John is not concerned to show Him to us as healer or teacher—that he can leave to the Evangelists. Rather, he is at pains to depict the Christ in glory. "No-where in the New Testament is the glory of the exalted Christ so emphasised", writes Dr. R. H. Charles. This Jesus, who still bears the tokens of His passion, is "the first-born from the dead and ruler of the kings of the earth" (1, 5). He is the coming one, whom every eye shall see (1, 7). To Him the prerogatives of deity are ascribed (e.g. 1, 17; 2, 23 which is a quotation from Jeremiah 17, 10 where the words refer to the Lord God). The throne which St. John sees is the throne of God and of the Lamb (22, 3), and worship ascends to the Lamb (5, 8 ff.). He is Lord of lords, and King of kings (17, 14; 19, 16).

St. John delights to speak of our Lord as the Lamb—the title occurs nearly thirty times in this book. Central to the whole book is the writer's doctrine of atonement. "The Lamb as it had been slain", whose wrath is the more fearful because of His very meekness; enthroned, glorified, His humanity taken up into Godhead; able for this very reason, to open the book whose secrets are otherwise hidden from the eyes of men; Himself the Light of the city as He is also the centre of the worship of its inhabitants—this is the Christ of the *Revelation*.

We have seen something of the Seer's philosophy of history, and of his doctrine of God and of Christ. Has he anything of importance to say about the Church? Indeed he has. Nor do we have to wait long to hear what he says. He introduces the subject in 1, 6, where he describes the Church not only as the object of Christ's love and as that which has been freed from its sins with His life-blood, but also as "a kingdom" or royal house, to serve as priests of His God and Father. The passage is similar to I Peter 2, 9, and both passages are dependent on Exodus 19, 6: "Ye shall be unto me a kingdom of priests, and an holy nation". Just as Israel, set free from Egypt, acquired a national life of its own, so the Church, loosed from its sins, constitutes a holy nation, a sacerdotal society all of whose members are to offer themselves, their worship, their all to God. This idea is taken up again in 5, 9–10: "Thou wast slain and by Thy blood hast purchased for God men of every tribe and language and people and nation; Thou hast made them a royal house, to serve God as priests; and they shall reign upon earth". Like Daniel's "saints of the Most High"

(Daniel 7, 22, 25, 27), they exercise rule. But their rule is not rule as men normally conceive it. They rule (22, 5) as slaves (22, 3) of God and of the Lamb, their sole task being to do Him worshipful service.

This is the true Israel, the consecrated people of God, as distinct from those "who claim to be Jews but are not" (2, 9: 3, 9). They are God's people who have borne their witness to Jesus (17, 6). Some, indeed, as in the superb vision of Chapter 7, 9 ff., have sealed their witness with their blood, and, having passed through the great oppression and washed their robes in the blood of the Lamb, stand before the throne of God and minister to Him day and night in His temple, exempt from the rigours of hunger, thirst and heat. They are described as having "emerged victorious from the fight with the Beast, its statue and the number which denotes its name" (15, 2), and these are the words they sing: "Great and marvellous are Thy works, Lord God Almighty; just and true are Thy ways, thou King of saints. Who shall not fear Thee, O Lord, and glorify Thy name? for thou only art holy: for all nations shall come and worship before Thee: for Thy judgments are made manifest" (15, 3b and 4). Others, like those to whom the seven letters of Chapters 2 and 3 are sent, bear their witness under the full duress of suspicion and persecution.

Chapter 11 is a difficult and in some ways an abstruse passage. This much, however, would seem to be clear: God's two witnesses, appointed to prophesy (v. 3), represent the Church in its capacity of the body which bears testimony to God. The witnesses are to be a light, as the Lord had said—hence the reference in verse 4 to the olive trees and lamps. They are dressed in sackcloth (v. 3), for their message was one of judgment, and eventually they will be killed (v. 7). Their Lord had met a similar fate outside the walls of a city named Jerusalem but which seemed to have more in common with Sodom or pagan Egypt than with the "joy of the whole earth" (v. 8). But that is not the end. Just as the stories of Moses and Elijah (who clearly seem to be in the writer's mind in this passage — see especially v. 6) indicate a supernatural end for both these heroes (Deuteronomy 34, 6 and II Kings 2, 11), so too the witnesses "go up to heaven in a cloud" (v. 12) — victory and life follow persecution and death. Here is the Church triumphant. Attention to and digestion of the word of God (ch. 10, 8ff.), witness to the word of God and readiness to suffer for that witness (ch. 11) — that was the primary task of the Church, as indeed it still is.

Of the Church as the Bride of Christ (21, 9) I shall have a little to say at the end of this chapter. What has already been said, however, is sufficient to show that this book has scattered throughout it quite a rich doctrine of the Church. These tiny persecuted minorities are very dear to the Lord of the Church, and the very apple of His eye.

I need only add a word on the doctrine of the certainty of divine judgement which occupies a great place in the *Revelation*. This doctrine, which has as its corollary the doctrine of human responsibility, is one which is preached all too little to-day. What emerges from this book with a kind of inexorable clarity is the fact that issues of eternal moment hang on whether or no a man "worships the Beast" (20, 4); that the judgement of the great white throne (20, 11 ff.) when the books are opened is the one great fact before which all others pale into insignificance.

Lastly, what is to be said of the final state of the blessed as it is depicted in the closing chapters of our book? Four things stand out clearly:

(i) *Renewal and peace.* The sea, which to a land-loving Hebrew spoke of turmoil and danger, is no more (21, 1). There is a new heaven and a new earth, the creation of Him who sat on the throne and said, "Behold! I am making all things new!" (21, 5). The creative and re-creative power of God, of which modern science is making us increasingly aware, has, as it were, reached the climax of its work.

(ii) *Intimacy of communion*. The nuptial element, which occupies so big a place in the Bible's description of God's relationship with His people, comes to a head in the Seer's description of the Bride, the wife of the Lamb (21, 2, 9; 22, 17). This daring terminology is, as we have seen, used in antithesis to the harlot Babylon—purity is contrasted with obscenity. But there is more to it than that—here is the intimacy of the love which exists between Christ and His Church; here is communion at its deepest.

(iii) *Community living*. The state of the blessed is depicted, not as "the flight of the alone to the Alone", but as a community living in peace and security together. It is a *city*. Its name is Jerusalem in antithesis to Babylon. But it is *new* Jerusalem, undefiled and so, in this respect, unlike the Jerusalem which had persecuted the prophets and killed the Lord (21, 2, 10 ff.). There is no need to close the gates against enemy invasion or thieves by night, for there is no night there (21, 25). It lies foursquare (21, 16), the square being to the Greek a symbol of perfection, and to the Hebrew, nurtured on Ezekiel's vision of the holy city, a symbol of work divinely perfected. This vast cube of a city "comes down from God out of heaven" (21, 10). It does not come about by the development of immanent processes already at work in human society. It is linked to the life and testimony of the Christian Church; it comes down from God. Had not Jesus said: "Fear not, little flock; it is your Father's good pleasure to *give* you the Kingdom" (St. Luke 12, 32)? So St. John sees the world, society organised without reference to God, finished, done, or rather, re-created. The new Jerusalem has arrived from God! So A. C. Welch (*The Psalter in Life, Worship and History*) writes of the Psalmists' view of history: "The psalter . . . is . . . saturated with the conviction that there is an end to which all human history is moving. It is the end which God has appointed for it and to which He means to bring all things" (p. 29). "The end . . . is something which God is not conceived as bringing in through the slow course of history and through the discipline of man, as men learn to share His purpose. It is rather something which He superinduces on history, in order to correct an errant world and to prevent it from returning to chaos . . ." (p. 31). The word "superinduce", which Welch uses more than once in this essay, is an interesting comment from the Psalmists' viewpoint on the Seer's "coming down from God out of heaven."

(iv) *Worship*. No Temple (21, 22)? Imagine a Jew thinking of society without a temple! It is a "calculated shock of surprise—St. John loves paradox . . . No Temple, no holy part separated from the rest, for it is all Temple, the expansion of the Holy of Holies itself." (H. Erskine Hill: *Mystical Studies in the Apocalypse*, p. 135). "Its Temple is the sovereign Lord God and the Lamb." So it is that the task of the inhabitants of this new community is to *worship*. "His servants shall worship Him, and they shall see His face" (22, 3, 4).

Bishop Stephen Neill, at the end of his book *Christian Holiness* (pp. 129–30), writes of the surprise which is a constant factor in the experience of any man who treads the road of holiness—surprise at God's forgiveness of him and patience with him. He concludes with words with which we may well end this chapter. "I am inclined to think that this astonishment will not end with our pilgrimage upon earth. I can imagine myself waking up one day in the home of the blessed, and saying to myself in astonishment, 'Now, how in the world do I come to be here?' I can also imagine myself meeting some of my friends, as I hope to do, in those blessed fields and saying to them, 'Well now, how in the world do you come to be here?' Perhaps we shall look at one another in mutual surprise. If you ask me what I expect to be the chief characteristic of that life that will follow, when we have come to the end of the road, and sin and sorrow and conflict are no more, I think that perhaps I would be inclined to reply, 'Astonishment', or to put it a little more precisely, 'Astonished joy'."

I do not think that the Bishop's thought is far removed from that of the Seer.